D0239666

PLACE IN RETURN BOX to remove this checkout from your record.
TO AVOID FINES return on or before date due.

DATE DUE	DATE DUE	DATE DUE
SEP 2 7 1993	MICHIGAN STATE UNIVERSITY LIBRARY	
229		
SEP 23	FEB 23 2003	
	WITHDRAWN	

...nal Computers
and the Adult Learner

Barry Heermann, *Editor*

Personal Computers and the Adult Learner

Barry Heermann, *Editor*

NEW DIRECTIONS FOR CONTINUING EDUCATION
GORDON G. DARKENWALD, *Editor-in-Chief*

Number 29, March 1986

Paperback sourcebooks in
The Jossey-Bass Higher Education Series

Jossey-Bass Inc., Publishers
San Francisco • London

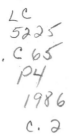

Barry Heermann (Ed.).
Personal Computers and the Adult Learner.
New Directions for Continuing Education, no. 29.
San Francisco: Jossey-Bass, 1986.

New Directions for Continuing Education Series
Gordon G. Darkenwald, *Editor-in-Chief*

New Directions for Continuing Education (publication number
USPS 493-930) is published quarterly by Jossey-Bass Inc., Publishers.
Second-class postage rates are paid at San Francisco, California,
and at additional mailing offices.

Correspondence:
Subscriptions, single-issue orders, change of address notices,
undelivered copies, and other correspondence should be sent
to Subscriptions, Jossey-Bass Inc., Publishers, 433 California Street,
San Francisco, California 94104.

Editorial correspondence should be sent to the Editor-in-Chief,
Gordon G. Darkenwald, Graduate School of Education, Rutgers
University, 10 Seminary Place, New Brunswick, New Jersey 08903.

Library of Congress Catalog Card Number 85-81882

International Standard Serial Number ISSN 0195-2242

International Standard Book Number ISBN 87589-711-8

Cover art by WILLI BAUM

Manufactured in the United States of America

Ordering Information

The paperback sourcebooks listed below are published quarterly and can be ordered either by subscription or single-copy.

Subscriptions cost $40.00 per year for institutions, agencies, and libraries. Individuals can subscribe at the special rate of $30.00 per year *if payment is by personal check.* (Note that the full rate of $40.00 applies if payment is by institutional check, even if the subscription is designated for an individual.) Standing orders are accepted.

Single copies are available at $9.95 when payment accompanies order, and *all single-copy orders under $25.00 must include payment.* (California, New Jersey, New York, and Washington, D.C., residents please include appropriate sales tax.) For billed orders, cost per copy is $9.95 plus postage and handling. (Prices subject to change without notice.)

Bulk orders (ten or more copies) of any individual sourcebook are available at the following discounted prices: 10–49 copies, $8.95 each; 50–100 copies, $7.96 each; over 100 copies, *inquire.* Sales tax and postage and handling charges apply as for single copy orders.

To ensure correct and prompt delivery, all orders must give either the *name of an individual* or an *official purchase order number.* Please submit your order as follows:

Subscriptions: specify series and year subscription is to begin.
Single Copies: specify sourcebook code (such as, CE1) and first two words of title.

Mail orders for United States and Possessions, Latin America, Canada, Japan, Australia, and New Zealand to:
Jossey-Bass Inc., Publishers
433 California Street
San Francisco, California 94104

Mail orders for all other parts of the world to:
Jossey-Bass Limited
28 Banner Street
London EC1Y 8QE

New Directions for Continuing Education
Gordon G. Darkenwald, *Editor-in-Chief*

Contents

Editor's Notes

The purpose of this sourcebook is to inform continuing education professionals in colleges and in training departments of corporations, government agencies, and other organizations about opportunities for enhancing educational processes with computers.

The impact of the personal computer in the wider society has been remarkable. By 1987 there will be an electronic keyboard for every white-collar worker (including keyboards that operate personal computers, terminals, electronic typewriters, word processors, and so on). The majority of these keyboards will operate personal computers ("Trends in Computing. . . ," 1984).

With this nearly universal adoption of the personal computer as the "workhorse" of the nation, adults find themselves immersed in new learning projects involving the use of the personal computer or the software that drives personal computers. These learning activities most often take the form of independent learning projects, conducted without institutional sponsorship.

Since the number of informal learning projects not sponsored by continuing education providers is significant, the widespread use of personal computers poses two questions for continuing educators: How can we support adults in learning about computers and computer software, and how can we enrich adult learning in general through the use of computers? Before we can answer these questions, we need to distinguish between "learning *about* computers" and "learning *with* computers."

"Learning *about* computers" encompasses both "learning about computers in preparation for careers in computing" and "learning about computers to enhance skills in a variety of careers." The initial use of the technology was in the preparation of adults for careers in computing and information processing, primarily using mainframes. As employment opportunities for computer operators and programmers mushroomed, continuing educators responded with career training, emphasizing, especially, the mastery of computer languages, like COBOL and Fortran. This use of the technology, which continues today, served as the primary curricular thrust throughout the 1970s.

The shift in focus, from "learning about computers in preparation for careers in computing" to "learning about computers to enhance skills in a variety of careers," was a direct result of the advent of the inexpensive yet powerful and versatile personal computer. Now, the continuing education curriculum that covered "learning about computers" has expanded to include "learning about personal computers" and "learning about applications (software) for personal computers."

1

Thus, continuing education in the realm of computers has begun serving a far larger and more heterogeneous group of adults. These adults are interested in using the technology to heighten their effectiveness in a vast array of jobs; they do not intend to pursue careers as programmers or system analysts. The focus in these continuing education courses is on basic computer literacy, understanding the keyboard, determining requirements in megabytes of power, and determining the advantages of hard disk versus floppy disk drives, among other topics.

This shift from preparing persons for careers in data processing to instruction in personal computing in order to enhance job performance in a breadth of careers represents the most significant realignment within the rubric of "learning about computers." However, another shift has also occurred. Within the subcategory of "learning about personal computers," those continuing education programs that are sensitive to adult learners have started to teach how to use popular software programs (in addition to how to operate the personal computer) in order to reach whole new populations of adults.

This reorientation from hardware to software has resulted in new courses and seminar offerings that teach word processing, spread-sheet, data-base, and decision support programs. These curricular applications represent the cutting edge of computer use in most continuing education programs, and they reflect the pressing need for personal-computer users in corporate and other organizational settings. Sherrill Amador's chapter on financing and marketing computers in continuing education illustrates this curricular thrust.

The most significant shift in continuing education's conception of the computer and learning for adults is just now beginning to take shape. It involves the movement from "learning *about* computers" to "learning *with* computers." The critical pedagogical shift is from using the computer as course content to using the computer as a vehicle for learning. This notion is far from new: There have been numerous experiments in the use of computer-aided instruction (CAI), primarily in adult basic education, PLATO courses involving the mainframe, and drill and practice of basic skills in developmental education. Now, however, there is a greatly expanded vision of "learning with computers" that goes beyond CAI; this vision, described in Chapter One, is the harbinger of things to come.

This phase is taking on importance as creative educators adapt inexpensive, off-the-shelf software to forward the development of problem-solving, writing, computational, creative, and analytical skills in a variety of areas of study offered in comprehensive continuing education programs. Beyond the creative use of these powerful new applications programs, there is evidence of increased use of off-the-shelf as well as locally produced CAI in colleges and corporations (see particularly chapters Three and Six).

These shifts in curriculum and categories of learning provide the background for each of the chapters in this sourcebook, with focus on "learning about computers" in various ramifications. Specifically, this sourcebook explores adult learning strategies for using the personal computer in continuing education, the logistics of establishing a computer laboratory, the opportunities for networking with computers, and the financial and marketing parameters of using computers in these ways. This volume also provides a close-up look at the personal computer in the learning environment of a major corporation, as well as a glimpse into a series of model programs in a variety of settings. It concludes with a synthesis and observations about the appropriate use of personal computers in continuing education.

Chapter One, which I have written, provides a thumbnail sketch of technological advancements in personal computers and looks at the extent to which personal computers are used in corporate training, in higher education generally, and in continuing education specifically. Special attention is paid to the primary modes of employing the personal computer as a resource for adult learners in continuing education in order to provide a sense of the possibilities for "learning with computers."

Chapter Two examines hardware and other considerations related to the establishment of the computer labaoratory. James Hollowood provides generic guidelines for establishing a computer facility that works for adult students. Hollowood challenges existing beliefs as he interweaves guidelines and principles for setting up a model facility.

Chapters Three through Seven illustrate five model applications of the personal computer in programs of continuing education. Each application is described by a practitioner involved with the model project. In Chapter Three, Andrea Warfield at Ferris State College describes her "high-tech/high-touch" course in management, which uses off-the-shelf, computer-based learning software in a unique consortium project. Next Craig Scanlan describes an exemplary pedagogical application of the personal computer in allied health continuing education. In Chapter Five, Sandra Ratcliff examines a unique program of legal education that incorporates personal computers. In Chapter Six, Susan Heermann and Suzanne Wagner, the vice-president of a new and rapidly growing corporation, tell how this company positioned computer-based training as the focus of their management development program. Finally, Harriet Cabell, in Chapter Seven, describes how learning contracts that incorporate computer learning elements using students' own personal computers are used at the University of Alabama New College.

In Chapter Eight, corporate trainers John Thomasson and Ronald Larsen of NCR Corporation examine "The Personal Computer as a Vehicle for Learning in the Workplace." They describe the wide array of NCR training offerings that incorporate personal computers. Their chapter looks at the personal computer not only as an effective resource for learning but also as a powerful resource for faculty engaged in instructional development.

In Chapter Nine, Sherrill Amador draws on her own successful experience at Southwestern College as she looks at the marketing and the resulting financial payoffs of continuing education offerings that involve the computer. Amador underscores the demand of organizations and individuals for "learning about software for personal computers" in her community college district, emphasizing various marketing and programmatic considerations related to serving this need. Chapter Ten, by Ben Davis and Catherine Marlowe, examines the implications of electronic networking and data-base services for adult learners. They explore the feasibility and ramifications of electronic networking and communication with other students and with faculty in a computer network and the implications of being able to access elaborate data bases in conducting research, writing essays, or preparing projects.

The final chapter, by Barry Sheckley, provides a synthesis of viewpoints expressed in this sourcebook, with particular regard for the three principal uses of the personal computer in continuing education discussed in Chapter One. Sheckley looks at concepts of teaching and learning, learner autonomy, and the diverse opportunities the personal computer provides for continuing education.

As you read this sourcebook, keep in mind that computers possess nothing, intrinsically, that ensures their usefulness as vehicles for adult learning. The computer is merely a box of electronics, albeit a very powerful and wonderful box of electronics. Adding the educational "something" that can emerge for adult learners by engaging with the personal computer is the challenge to continuing education administrators and faculty.

Barry Heermann
Editor

Reference

"Trends in Computing Systems and Services for the '80s." *Fortune*, Special Supplement, July 9, 1984, pp. 1–64.

Barry Heermann is executive director of the Higher Education Management Institute, producer of Thoughtware computer-assisted education programs, and coordinator of educational consortiums experimenting with the personal computer as a resource for adult learners.

*Continuing educators can choose from a variety of
learning strategies, including using the computer as
a "teaching machine," a "learning resource," and a
"tool" for applied learning.*

Strategies for Adult
Computer Learning

Barry Heermann

This chapter explores the primary strategies for using personal computers
in continuing education. First, however, it provides a cursory review of
several major developments in computer technology, continuing education's response, and several observations about the possibilities for adult
learners equipped with personal computers. The distinction between
"learning about computers" and "learning with computers" made in the
Editor's Notes will serve as the background for this chapter, as strategies
for "learning with computers" will be explored.

The Context

A variety of telecommunication delivery modes were to have revolu-
tionized education in general, and continuing education in particular, in
the 1970s. They did not. Why should the personal computer be different?
The difference is that most of our major institutions now employ

The practical illustrations cited throughout this chapter are based on my
own consultation visits or have been excerpted from a collection of reports on
programs that have pioneered the educational uses of the computer, including a
report from the Fund for the Improvement of Postsecondary Education called
Computers in Education: Strategies and Resources (n.d.) and from an IBM publication entitled *Agenda: Academic Information Systems* (1985). Examples of practice
taken from other sources will be identified in the text.

B. Heermann (Ed.). *Personal Computers and the Adult Learner.*
New Directions for Continuing Education, no. 28. San Francisco: Jossey-Bass, March 1986.

personal computers to accomplish their work, especially in the business and scientific realms. The extent of this change is truly remarkable; by the end of this decade over half of all white-collar workers (35 million persons) will routinely use a personal computer ("Personal Computing: The Challenge to Management," 1985). "Learning about personal computers" and "learning about software" are currently among America's preeminent learning projects, involving millions of persons.

The adoption of the personal computer by the wider society is the result of its remarkable utility and low cost in doing the work of our information-rich culture. This utility will continue to increase, due to ongoing technological enhancements. Consider these advances in computer technology:

1. Computing power is increasing at the rate of about 25 percent each year ("Trends in Computing Systems and Services for the '80s," 1984).

2. Computing power that cost one million dollars in 1970 will cost only ten thousand dollars in 1990 ("Trends in Computing Systems and Services for the '80s." 1984).

3. In the next ten years, personal computers should increase in power tenfold while decreasing in price by 20 percent ("Personal Computing: The Challenge to Management," 1985).

4. Very shortly, personal computers will be readily available that are more powerful than the IBM 360 mainframe computer, announced two decades ago ("Trends in Computing Systems and Services for the '80s," 1984).

5. In the mid 1970s the two-kilobyte chip was news, today 256 kilobytes (K) is common and 512K chips are sought after for serioius home, study, and business use. And 1,000K chips will be here in the near future ("Trends in Computing Systems and Services for the '80s," 1984).

6. The computer will continue to shrink in size: from mainframe to mini, from mini to micro; micros will give way to portables; and portables will ultimately lead to pocket-sized computers.

These technological advances in personal-computer technology simplify and enhance the performance and effectiveness of organizations and individuals in performing informational and intellectual tasks. Accordingly, the widespread adoption of the personal computer by most major sectors of the society has prompted continuing educators to help adults learn about computers and software and, for the more pioneering, to help adults learn *with* computers. Consider how extensively the personal computer is being used in collegiate, corporate, and other training settings, as well as by higher education generally:

1. Fifty percent of Fortune 500 companies currently use computer-assisted training (Zemke, 1984).

2. Higher education spends $100 billion annually on computers (Kindel and Benoit, 1984).
3. In the four-year period from 1981 to 1985, the number of personal computers on campuses grew from under 25,000 to approximately 375,000, a fifteenfold increase in utilization (Kindel and Benoit, 1984).
4. Thirty-six percent of all trainers in organizations with fifty or more employees are computer-assisted training (Zemke, 1984).
5. Nearly 500,000 personal computers should be in place on campuses in 1987 (Turner, 1984).

Moreover, students themselves are leading the move to expand use of personal computers in colleges and universities:

1. In 1987 student ownership of personal computers will exceed institutional ownership eight times (Turner, 1984).
2. Twenty percent of adult learners could be using computers in their instructional programs in higher education in the near future (Meierhenry, 1982).
3. In 1987 some four million students will own their own personal computer (Turner, 1984).
4. From 1982 to 1983 alone the number of students who owned personal computers tripled from about 250,000 to 750,000 (Turner, 1984).

The impact of the personal computer is reflected in a vast array of applications in continuing education. The computer can serve as a patient tutor for the statistician, a challenging simulator for the engineer, a writing assistant for the aspiring poet, an analytical tool for the geologist, or the communications link that allows the student of management to "talk" with managerial peers.

In each of these examples, the use of computers has resulted in subtle but important changes in the way adults learn. For example, computers help adults initiate and direct learning activities without the direct supervision of faculty members. Consequently, computers also allow learners greater ownership of the learning process. The shift from passive learning (I learn from a book or a faculty member) to more active learning (I learn from engagement or application using the computer as the vehicle) heralds a shift in the teaching-learning process.

Because the personal computer promotes active learning, it allows a more effective integration of theory and practice. The problem orientation that the computer can facilitate causes adult learners to grapple with strategies for achieving results, drawing on and integrating principles and theory learned through classroom processes in order to apply them to real-world or simulated contexts.

However, making the computer the sole or primary vehicle for learning misuses the technology. There is some optimal gestalt of faculty lectures, group interaction, and computer-enhanced activities. "Learning with computers" can heighten continuing education learning outcomes, but only to the extent that it is considered alongside such factors as the intended interpersonal nature of the classroom process and the desired computer environment.

Adult learners need and want opportunities for regular and meaningful interaction with peers, as well as support and feedback from teachers. Computers can actually contribute to an enhancement of group interactions, freeing up time for in-class sharing and discovery.

In Chapter Two, Hollowood draws on his experience with the Harvard Extension computer facility. He not only looks at the campus facility but also points to the opportunities beyond the campus for adult learners who have access to personal computers at their work sites. Thus, the notion of the computer environment needs to be thought of expansively for continuing education students. Currently, adult learners are engaging in computing in the community, at work, and at home, in addition to on campus. And these noncampus locations are especially important to keep in mind in designing facilities and instructional experiences, as some computer work may be completed at the learner's own computer. In Chapter Seven, Cabell describes the use of learning contracts as a means to engage learners with their work-based personal computers.

Learning Strategies for Using Computers

A distinction was made in the Editor's Notes between "learning about computers" and "learning with computers." "Learning about computers" continues to evolve beyond its original programming focus and now includes a wider audience and broader definition of what "computer literacy" entails. Whether bringing the operational use of a personal computer or software to the rural poor or offering advanced courses in computer applications to corporate managers, the basic work of disseminating information about computers will continue to be a focus of continuing education.

This kind of instruction, however, represents only the tip of the iceberg. Creative faculty working with adult learners are increasingly using personal computers to enhance learning processes across a broad spectrum of subject areas. Thus, "learning with computers" offers an expanding range of opportunities for continuing educators.

Regardless of subject area, there are essentially three basic educational strategies for learning with computers in continuing education. These three strategies encompass the personal computer as a tool, a resource, and a teaching machine.

In programs that emphasize "learning with computers" versus "learning about computers," the personal computer is best understood as the background from which learning can emerge in the foreground. Decisions about the use of the computer must result from a learner-centered versus computer-centered philosophy. The particular learning styles of adults, the circumstances of learning, the discipline of study, and the intended outcomes of the learning experience will dictate which strategies or combinations of strategies will be most appropriate. These strategies and the many possible combinations of them suggest a variety of ways to serve learners.

Using the Computer as a Tool. A major barrier to the use of personal computers in the continuing education curriculum has stemmed from a concern about the development cost of software and the reluctance of faculty to engage in such development. The current breakthrough is in the form of inexpensive yet powerful off-the-shelf software programs that can be used creatively to enrich the learning experience in a diverse array of continuing education offerings.

Highly sophisticated, commercially available software can assist learners in computation, research, problem solving, analysis, writing, and creative thinking. Word processing, graphing, idea-generation, data-base, and spread-sheet programs developed for managerial applications in business and industry can be used effectively by continuing educators.

The largest single use of the computer in colleges and universities is not computer-aided instruction (CAI), as is popularly assumed; it is for word processing (Turner, 1984). Word processing software amounted to one fourth of the $1.3 billion expended for all software in 1984 by all organizations worldwide (*InfoWorld*, 1985). Consider these uses of off-the-shelf software:

1. Physics students equipped with spread-sheet programs are able to focus on the principles of physics rather than on the calculus customarily needed to learn physics. The effect is that a much wider audience of students is able to complete the course.
2. Evening students of geology use a popular filing program to create data bases of common minerals, identifying their qualities, and entering data about their special properties.
3. Students of economics record and analyze key economic indicators for a particular underdeveloped nation.
4. Radiology students use a popular spread-sheet program to perform calculations, make comparisons, and prepare lab reports.
5. Students of early childhood education use a data-base program to record historical data for preschoolers enrolled in a local program.
6. Sociology students use data management and graphing programs to collect, graph, and analyze particular demographic data for various suburban areas surrounding a major metropolitan city.
7. Marketing students use a graphing program to plot market-penetration data for a series of product lines.

Using the Computer as a Resource. Yet another useful strategy for using the computer is as a "resource" for learners. The distinction between "tool" and "resource" that is suggested here is like that between a hammer or a saw, on the one hand, and a telephone or an encyclopedia, on the other. That is, the computer as a tool assists the learner as an instrument to perform some task or analytical work, while the computer as a resource makes available a supply of information and a means of communication.

The computer used as a resource is like a communication facilitator; it connects the adult learner with the relevant resources, using a communication device (that is, a modem), so that the learner can complete some project or research. Computer conferencing, faculty-learner bulletin boards, and on-line data-base services are examples of using the computer as a resource.

Further examples include the New York Institute of Technology and TeleLearning, the "electronic university," which delivers on-line credit and noncredit courses to homes and businesses in collaboration with a diverse set of colleges and universities ("A Wizard's Plan for an 'Electronic University,' " 1984; Glossbrenner, 1984).

Both TeleLearning and the New York Institute of Technology represent an intermingling of the computer as teaching machine and as resource. Another institutional example is the University of Illinois and its development of a medical "textbook" in pathology that serves at once as a continuing education system and an elaborate information bank for students of pathology (Balestri and others, 1984).

Memphis State University established a data base on research and curricular materials about minority and working-class women in the South and uses the clearinghouse to facilitate awareness about these particular women's issues. Here, special information is accessible as never before.

The University of Michigan developed the community Classroom-Telephone-Computer (CTC) Learning Network for Fundamental Reasoning Skills. Access was available to anyone in the community by phone.

Finally, corporate executives engage in a wide variety of computer conferences focused on managerial issues, problems, and concerns and are able to retrieve stock-market quotations as well as determine flight schedules for commuting to business meetings.

Using the Computer as a Teaching Machine. The image of the computer as a teaching machine, transmitting knowlege through interactive and engaging presentations, is the most popular and widely referred to of its uses. But with the unusual utility of applications programs (that allow the computer to be used as a tool) and with the increased use of the computer as a resource for accessing data and for communicating, the computer as a teaching machine no longer occupies a place of prominence. This is due in large part to the relatively limited availability of educational software and to the cost of developing locally produced software.

The biggest exception to this generalization is in corporate and other training settings where computer-assisted training is occupying a position of increasing importance. This is suggested in the descriptions of corporate programs at NCR (Chapter Eight) and Cernitin (Chapter Six).

The popular conception of the teaching machine is embodied in computer-aided instruction (CAI), which subsumes both drill and practice, and tutorials. CAI is simply defined as the automation of programmed learning, in which behavioral objectives are reinforced with highly linear presentations.

Drill and Practice. The most common form of CAI is drill and practice. Mathematics can usefully be taught through drill and practice. For example, a basic algebra program might present the problem "$17 \times ab = ?$" on the video display. The response "17ab" might receive the message, "Congratulations." Or an incorrect response might receive the message, "Sorry, try again."

Good drill-and-practice programming, however, goes well beyond highly linear presentations of rote skills reviewed with simplistic questions. Otherwise, the programs justly deserve the criticism of Eric Ashby (1974):

> The weakness of programmed instruction is that it not only rewards rote learning but, and worse than that, it rewards only those responses which are in agreement with the programme. . . . Anyone with an original mind can get no stimulus or satisfaction out of the programme. Furthermore, the declared aim of those who compose programmes is to make the steps so simple that the learner does not make mistakes, and so gets his reinforcement at every step; but making mistakes is an essential experience in learning. . . [p. 37].

Tutorials. This computer learning mode involves a step-by-step presentation of principles and theory. It provides for practice of those principles, asks questions for comprehension, and assigns instruction based on the response. A good program may adapt to the learner's skill levels, branching to other appropriate material.

Critics of continuing education have argued that traditional classroom teaching has relied far too heavily on fact transmission to teach subject matter that is often largely interpersonal in content (such as psychology, management, social work, or education). Because of the computer's unusual capacity to process data, there is the clear risk that information related to such disciplines could all too easily be transferred to the computer, precluding direct contact with the interpersonal basis of the discipline. Knowing the principles of problem solving, entrepreneurship, and communications will never substitute for direct experience in solving problems, advancing ideas, or communicating. The opportunity for enrichment lies in deciding what data should be conveyed on the computer, freeing class time for meaningful personal interaction. With such a balance (and perhaps offered in conjunction with some relevant off-campus internship), adult learners can develop the necessary interpersonal skills. In addition, using CAI in conjunction with using the computer as a tool exploits the computer's ability to process student-generated data from their own experiments and experiences.

A significant number of people learn best through nonsequential and experiential processes versus abstraction or logical, linear presentation. Gueulette (1982) observes that "recent research has indicated that perhaps as much as one half of the population has the sort of cognitive structure that resists acquisition of knowledge from the highly linear and orderly process of the computer" (p. 181). Note that implicit in Gueulette's assessment is the image of the computer as a teaching machine versus the computer as a learning resource or tool.

The computer as a teaching machine may never be appropriate for some persons. The computer used as a tool or a learning resource, in more active learning contexts, is more congruent and thus effective for many adults having learning styles oriented toward direct experience.

Ashby (1974) cautions that "we must be patient"; we are at an early stage in the development of the computer as a teaching machine, comparable to Gutenberg's first book or Daimler's first automobile. He reminds us of the unexplored possibilities that may result in the development of "really sophisticated machines which could conduct a dialogue with the student and not merely reward him when he gives the orthodox response" (p. 37). Thus, while CAI is currently the predominant notion of the teaching machine, there are new assessment, modeling, testing, and managed-instruction offshoots of CAI that suggest something of the future for the computer in continuing education.

Personal Assessment. The computer can promote personal awareness. This is evidenced in career-counseling software configured for adults, such as SIGI Plus and Discover for Adults, which encourage students to clarify their values, skills, and other personal attributes in order to clarify personal and career intentions.

A recent project has combined this sort of assessment with the content for an introductory psychology course. The University of Illinois uses computers to teach undergraduate psychology, employing a self-discovery approach wherein students use a personal computer to conduct a series of experiments on themselves. Each module is designed to reveal an aspect of mental functioning that would not otherwise be obvious to the student but that is fundamental to modern psychological theory. Phenomena that would otherwise seem abstract and distant become concrete and personal.

Other examples are software produced by the Leading Edge and diagnostic programs produced by Thoughtware (including "Management Advantage") that cause persons to reflect on their skills and abilities in various managerial and communication situations. Both of these programs underscore the potential of the computer to provide private and immediate feedback to adults, increasing their awareness.

Simulations. Simulations involve learners in explorations of relationships among social or physical variables under artificial conditions that model reality. Learners experience events and explore relationships that would normally be too expensive or too time-consuming to provide. The most popular example is the flight simulator, which allows adults to experience the realities of flying and landing an airplane. Other applications include business games, genetic models, simulated machinery, and numerous other artificial renderings of phenomena.

The University of Wisconsin introduced a course in nuclear plant dynamics into the nuclear engineering curriculum based on a simple but realistic plant simulator running on IBM PC/AT computers. It will help to increase safety in nuclear power plants through training engineers to a greater intuitive understanding of plant dynamics.

Other experiments in the use of computerized simulations for academic purposes are being carried out at the University of Maryland (optics), Southern Illinois University (environmental factors), and Washington State University (physiology).

Student Testing. Evaluation conducted on the computer can provide for test-item generation (typically multiple choice), administration of testing, grading, reporting, and the recording or transcripting of the learner's performance. As in all evaluation, the intention is to determine the learner's progress in achieving educational goals. In addition, the computer can provide prescriptions for additional learning activities, including text or reading assignments, laboratory work, other academic projects, or some form of individualized computer-aided study.

Computer-Managed Instruction (CMI). CMI is a field in and of itself. Subsumed in CMI are all of the administrative tasks that undergird CAI, including evaluations of student performance, record keeping, and resource utilization (such resources as carrels, terminals, and so on). Related to record keeping is the scheduling of projects and activities, the organization of curricula, and the recording of individual and group performance. Howard Community College in Maryland has implemented a system of computer-managed instruction that supports its instruction-by-objectives learning process. The system helps the instructor design the course and analyze learner progress, while providing information to learners that allows them to proceed at their own pace.

Importance of the Teacher

Regardless of the strategies used to exploit the computer's power in the continuing education program, the importance of the teacher to the teaching-learning process is as great as ever. The task of arranging meaningful learning resources, one component of which is the personal computer, will require creative faculty perspectives about the time and space dimensions of its use.

Lectures have historically served to inspire and illuminate. The personal computer without the guidance of a concerned faculty will almost surely fail to provide the motivation and personal dynamic required to support adult learners in achieving desired learning outcomes. Consider this admonition by Ashby (1974):

> Five centuries of the printed book have not diminished the need for the lecture, seminar, and tutorial. In most fields of knowledge—even in science and technology—the intuitive value judgment, the leap of imagination, and the processing of data by analogy rather than by deduction, are characteristic of the best kind of education. We know no way to elicit these except through dialogue between the teacher and the pupil. The most precious qualities transmitted from teacher to pupil are not facts and theories, but attitudes of mind and styles of thinking [p. 39].

In conclusion, the computer as a "tool," a "learning resource," and a "teaching machine" only imperfectly mirrors continuing education practice. There are hybrid programs that encompass the computer as a "tool" and a "resource" (for example, data bases and word-processing programs, or tools, accessed through a network, or resource), or combinations of the "teaching machine" and the "resource" as exemplified in a CAI program (teaching machine) used in juxtaposition with a faculty-student bulletin board (resource). The "spaces" *between* these basic learning strategies offer particularly interesting possibilities for creating new permutations and combinations of services.

Continuing education is at a unique point in its development as technological breakthroughs touch every aspect of adult life in America. Continuing education's options for imaginatively serving adults with alternative learning strategies that employ the computer are each day becoming more varied and more compelling. The remainder of this volume will serve to clarify some of the possibilities open to continuing education.

References

Agenda: Academic Information Systems—University AEP Conference. Milford, Conn.: IBM, 1985.

Ashby, E. *Adapting Universities to a Technological Society.* San Francisco: Jossey-Bass, 1974.

"A Wizard's Plan for an 'Electronic University.' " *Business Week.* March 19, 1984, p. 60.

Balestri, D., Cochrane, H., and Thrush, D. "High Tech, Low Tech, No Tech: Three Case Studies of Computers in the Classroom." *AAHE Bulletin.* December 1984, pp. 11-14.

Fund for the Improvement of Postsecondary Education. *Computers in Education: Strategies and Resources—The FIPSE Technology Study Group.* Washington D.C.: Fund for the Improvement of Postsecondary Education, n.d.

Glossbrenner, A. "On-Line College." *PC Magazine,* October 30, 1984, pp. 297-299.

Gueulette, D. G. (Ed.) *Microcomputers for Adult Learning.* Chicago, Ill.: Follett, 1982.

InfoWorld, April 29, 1985, p. 36.

Kindel, S., and Benoit, E. "Hello, Mr. Chip," *Forbes.* April 23, 1984, pp. 132-135.

Meierhenry, W. C. "Microcomputers and Adult Learning." *Training and Development Journal.* December 1982, pp. 58-66.

"Personal Computing: The Challenge to Management." *Forbes.* Special Supplement, 1985, pp. 1-34.

"Trends in Computing—Systems and Services for the '80s." *Fortune.* Special Supplement, July 9, 1984, pp. 1-64.

Turner, J. A. "Notes on Computers." *The Chronicle of Higher Education.* May 23, 1984, p. 15.

Zemke, R. "Evaluating Computer-Assisted Instruction: The Good, The Bad, and The Why." *Training.* May 1984, pp. 22-47.

Barry Heermann is executive director of the Higher Education Management Institute, producer of Thoughtware computer-assisted education programs, and coordinator of educational consortiums experimenting with the personal computer as a resource for adult learners.

A wide range of microcomputer hardware issues, space considerations, and scheduling guidelines must be addressed in order to create personal computer facilities that meet the needs of continuing education students.

Designing Microcomputer Facilities for Continuing Education

James R. Hollowood

Design of microcomputer facilities requires the careful synthesis of both curricular aims and resources. This is particularly true for continuing education students, most of whom are working adults. The selection of microcomputer hardware is always a compromise between the practical needs of students and the available budget. Hardware discounts provided by various vendors are weighed against compatibility needs. Software selections should include packages useful to the adult learner on the job; they should also expand the adult student's understanding of information technology, immediate practicality notwithstanding. A third software issue is its ability to support the curriculum.

Once the broad hardware and software questions are addressed, there are many hardware details that demand attention. These include the need for static reduction devices, the use of glare-free screens, and printer selection, for example. Space is another important consideration. Facilities should include spaces for the microcomputer room, the software storage and distribution functions, software demonstrations, and more traditional classroom and library activities. The most productive use of teaching and technical staff is a major challenge as well. With the working adult, time

B. Heermann (Ed.). *Personal Computers and the Adult Learner.*
New Directions for Continuing Education, no. 29. San Francisco: Jossey-Bass, March 1986.

is of great importance. The use of the student's time must be carefully examined. The scheduling of access to facilities, hardware, software, and staff is critical.

Early specification of design assumptions is strongly suggested if not mandatory. The obvious first question is what will be taught—which courses will the microcomputer facility support? The teaching of broad-based information technology and microcomputing will suggest one design. A specific focus on business applications will suggest a second design, while a general education focus will call for a third. Of course, software selections will influence hardware needs as well.

A second assumption relates to computer use: how many courses, how many students, how many hours per week. With working adults, you need to estimate the number and time of computer facility visits. Do the students have easy access to the facility and want to "pop in" during lunch hours, or will the students use the facility chiefly during the evening and weekend hours?

A related consideration is the availability of other computers either at home or in the workplace. While the use of other hardware and software resources usually cannot be mandated, continuing education students will use these "extra" resources if available, thereby taking some pressure off the school's microcomputer facility.

There are also a number of design assumptions that relate to teaching style. One instructional style may call for the extensive use of demonstrations. Another may rely on self-learning with periodic question-and-answer sessions. Yet another approach may call for tutorials offered in the computer room with the students working with the machines.

The following sections look at each of these considerations in detail and offer guidelines for creating a microcomputer facility to meet specific needs.

General Hardware and Software Issues

While conventional wisdom suggests that we should determine software requirements before considering hardware, hardware decisions are often made prior to a full explication of software. There are several good reasons for this practice. Many educational institutions are already associated with a hardware vendor and are willing to trade precise hardware requirements for assumed compatibility among levels or sizes of hardware. Maintaining a consistent business relationship with the hardware vendor is also important. Those institutions not tied to a particular hardware vendor often find that a range of salespeople offers money-saving deals or arrangements. When opportunity knocks, it is usually wise to accept significant cost savings.

A third reason for hardware being put before software is that faculty, particularly in schools just beginning to use computers, do not always know what software will be used. Even if one knows what software should be used now, the situation often changes. Budgetary constraints will often change the best of plans, and faculty will find they must use what is available, not what was intended or wanted. And, most important, software available on the market will change from month to month. While hardware may be expected to last for several years, only the very wise or very foolish will forecast the software picture two years or even one year hence.

Another reality is the "contagious" nature of computers in most settings. This year one group of faculty is ready to use the computer with specific software needs. Next year the second wave creates a new set of software requirements, and so on for the third and fourth years. Thus, there are many good reasons for putting the proverbial cart before the horse.

The "Best" Hardware. It can be argued that institutions ought to use the hardware employed by those organizations providing jobs for graduates. While this is accurate to a point, business, industry, and service organizations should not be assumed to have superior hardware knowledge or solutions. In addition, what a firm plans or does one year may very well change the next. Educators, true to their societal purpose, can and should question the claims of all hardware vendors. Through the educational process, research, and public service, educational institutions are expected to lead, not follow. Continuing educators should try, test, and question the purposes and performance of various types and brands of hardware. This does not imply that each program should try to support six or seven different computers. However, educators should carefully weigh their responsibility to lead both students and society toward a greater knowledge of computer use.

Compatibility. Another general issue is compatibility and its close ally, availability. It is comforting to know that one has a computer that will run thousands of software packages. The more important question, however, is which ten, twelve, or fiffteen software packages will be used? Almost all major and many minor hardware vendors have machines that will run all the software that a continuing education program could reasonably manage.

A more important question might be the continued availability of the hardware. Determine if the hardware will be supported by the company and if the company will be in business in two or three years. Give less attention to numbers of software packages and greater attention to the need for hardware support and maintenance over the life of the machine— say three or four years.

The question of compatibility has several dimensions. If the computers being purchased must be integrated with the computers already owned by the institution—then compatibility is an issue. In this case, all potential hardware vendors should be required to demonstrate that their solution to your microcomputer needs is in fact integrated. At the same time, it should be noted that the need for machines used for instruction to be fully integrated with another set of machines is much lower in educational than in business and industrial environments. While the need for integration is growing, most institutions will realize full useful service of their current computers before this need for integration becomes too pressing.

A related but more important question is software compatibility among various computing sites—school, home, and work. Almost every student has access to a different word processing program. The solution is using word processing assignments that are generic and can be completed with almost any word processing package. The opportunity, from the perspective of many students, is that they can learn the package used at work and also try the alternative used by the school. The same is true for data-base packages. Many students have access to packages that may or may not be what the continuing education program uses, hardware compatibility notwithstanding. A similar solution, in terms of assignments, may be possible, but the point is that compatibility encompasses both hardware and software considerations.

Upgrading. Another aspect of the issues of hardware compatibility and software availability is what may be called upgrading. Put simply, computer hardware and software are constantly and quickly being improved, enhanced, and expanded. Continuing education programs, if they are to remain current, must move with these trends. For example, a program's hardware and software are of little consequence if the firms who will employ graduates are using graphics while the students are perfecting their ability to generate ever more rows and columns of numbers with a spread sheet. If the program has the same machine as local business but only half the memory, it is significantly limited in what can be taught. In short, upgrading computers to contemporary standards is a most important consideration.

Specific Hardware Issues

Deciding How Many Computers to Buy. One popular question is the number of microcomputers that should be purchased. Should the number be one for every fifty students, one for each group of thirty, or one for ten? The answer, of course, depends on how many hours per week the machines are available and how many computer-hours each student will be expected to generate.

At one school, the microcomputer labs are open for continuing education use from 4:00 P.M. until midnight weekdays and from 9:00 A.M. until 10:00 P.M. weekends. This gives some sixty-six hours of available computer time per week per computer. The school then estimates the number of students hours of computer time required by the various courses and does the arithmetic that results in the number of computers needed. For example, the school planned to use computers in six courses that would collectively generate an approximate 900 student computer-hours per week. With sixty-six hours per week per machine, the number of computers needed was calculated to be fourteen. The school then made an allowance for malfunctioning machines and some expansion in the use of the machines and purchased eighteen microcomputers.

Another institution has fifteen machines for about 200 students who are estimated to generate some 600 student computer-hours per week in sixty hours of available time. A third has fifteen machines for some seventy students who are expected to generate approximately 700 student computer-hours per week in fifty hours of available time. As a rule of thumb, the student computer-hours work out to be about 70 to 80 percent of the total computer-hours available.

Availability During Peak Periods. One could argue that this calculation underestimates the number of machines needed because of peak load hours. This has not been found to be a problem; the diversity of adult students' schedules results in the machines being used about the same at all hours without serious complaint.

If peak loading does present a problem, one should then lower the hours of machine availability to the actual number of student computer-hours needed and recalculate the result. It can be argued that adult continuing education students operate on a tight schedule, making peak loading a certain and serious problem. Again, several schools have not found this to be so. While continuing education students, working adults in particular, do operate on a tight schedule, they are often flexible and adaptive in setting that schedule. As a group, they seem to distribute themselves across the hours of computer availability very well.

Availability of Outside Computers. An important question is how many students use computers at home or at work and thereby reduce the load on the institution's machines. Judging from the experience of several schools, that number is large and quickly growing. As an example, of the seventy adult students in one introductory microcomputer course, at least forty had access to a computer at home or work. However, this does not permit reducing the estimated number of school computers by half. While students may have access to an outside machine, they may not have access to the software being used in the various courses. For example, if students are required to use a specific word processing package, the load on the school's computers is likely to be high. However, if any word processing package is acceptable for the assignment, then students will be able to use computers at home or work. It is more reasonable then, to reduce the estimated number of school computers by, say, 20 or 25 percent as a result of outside computer use.

Summary of Computer-Need Considerations. In general, one can approximate the number of microcomputers needed with common sense and simple arithmetic. The peak load factor must be considered but is usually not a serious problem. Given a reasonably broad range of available hours, adult continuing education students will sort themselves out reasonably well. An increasing number of students have access to outside computers, and this may help reduce the peak load as well as overall requirements for school-owned microcomputers. Of equal importance to the numbers are the software used and flexibility of assignments. The more popular the software and the more flexible the assignments, the lesser the load or demand for school computer use. Each of these factors should be used to adjust the initial approximation of microcomputer needs. Of course, each continuing education program must weigh its own particular circumstances as well. It is probably safe to argue that one should err on the low side and then adjust upwards as local conditions warrant.

Deciding on the Size and Power of Microcomputers. Another set of important questions has to do with the size and power of microcomputers required by continuing education students. If a school plans to provide the most elementary level of computer training, so-called home computers in the $300 to $500 range may suffice. While this type of machine is slow and limited in versatility, it will permit the teaching of a few programming languages like BASIC and a number of elementary word processing applications.

Another alternative is the computer of larger but still modest size and power. A number of more sophisticated home computers that can double as very small business machines will cost between $1,000 and $1,500 and will support a respectable range of software. For general education, these machines will use various programming languages, word processors, modest graphics, and a variety of specially developed educational programs. They will also run a number of math and statistical programs but generally will not support larger packages used for teaching and major research projects.

However, there are two major notes of caution to be mentioned here. The more modern and more powerful software can easily demand more computer power than these machines were designed to deliver. The question, then, is how important is it for an instructional program to be state of the art. If it is important, then these smaller computers will probably not be a good investment.

The second caution is closely related to the first. No matter how small one starts there will be pressure to grow, to equip the computer lab with more powerful equipment. While small machines will handle some expansion, the more important question is price. By the time these machines are upgraded, they often result in a greater investment than having purchased a more powerful computer in the first place.

The most popular and commonly purchsed machine is the $2,500 variety (examples include the IBM PC and the Apple Macintosh). This machine normally has 256,000 bytes of memory, two floppy disk drives, and significant capacity for expansion. More often than not, these computers do not have graphics or color capability, which is an increasingly serious problem. These machines will support almost all general education and business requirements for the average continuing education program. Of course, if the program wants to support more sophisticated research and statistical programs, a hard disk at significant extra cost will be required. What is usually more important is assuring that these machines will support the purposes for which they were purchased. If the school buys the basic "256K box" but does not fully equip it, a better buy might have been the less expensive model discussed above. To maintain state-of-the-art computers that run present and emerging software, you will have to upgrade the basic machines. This usually requires additional memory, which is relatively inexpensive. In fact, memory has become, in a word, cheap. It could be argued that not to purchase the add-on memory is to be penny wise and pound foolish.

The same is true for graphics; with so many programs, existing and emerging, that use graphics, it is almost obligatory to purchase the graphics option with all computers, particularly those used for business and management software. Color options, such as color monitors, are less important. Many of the more popular programs can use color options and an increasing number require both color and graphics options; however, most of the popular programs can be run with or without color. A reasonable compromise is to equip the machines with color options but not necessarily to purchase the color monitors, which can be too expensive to justify the added benefit. An exception to this general rule is the continuing education program that wants to promote the significant use of graphics in computer and other courses. In this case, the program will want to use the more sophisticated graphics programs—those used for both business and general education—and they require color monitors for full power and utilization.

The more recent microcomputers, the "super minis" as they are sometimes called, also merit mention. These machines, depending on how they are configured, can cost between $4,000 and $7,000 and generally will do all that would be required by a continuing education program. They usually have one to one and one-half million bytes of memory and a hard disk of ten to twenty megabytes. They will probably have graphics and color capabilities as well. The problem at this time is that these machines with multiuser operating systems do not run all the popular software—a proble.n that probably will be corrected relatively soon. Thus, if one is buying for the short term, these machines would be a less-than-adequate choice, but the educational program planning for the future—two or three years away—may do well to consider the super minis.

Deciding on Communications Capabilities. In addition to the type of computers purchased, there are several smaller but related issues. The first of these is the need for a communications capability to make possible the use of the computer as a "learning resource," as discussed in Chapter One. One could assert the importance of using electronic mail, data communications, downloading of data files, and print serving on a central host computer. These capabilities, however, are expensive and difficult to implement. Of course, the theory and concepts of data communications can and should be taught. But the fact remains that some of these issues are technical ones not often addressed by the average user. Of importance to most microcomputer users is how to use data communications once the technology is in place. Learning how to use a particular communications system is often better left until students are on the job and can address the specifics of their organization's system.

Deciding on Printers and Plotters. Another important question involves the purchase of printers. To buy or not to buy printers is not the issue; they are essential. The question is how many printers should be purchased. One rule of thumb is one printer for every four machines. Microcomputers are usually arranged in squares of four with one printer serving the cluster through the use of a mechanical switch box. Increasingly however, the norm is becoming one printer for each two computers, again by means of a mechanical switching arrangement.

Related to printers are graphic plotters, which many of the more sophisticated graphics programs will support if not require. The question is, how necessary is it for teaching purposes to use a color plotter versus getting the same capability through lower-quality output on a monochrome or color printer? The answer, for now, is that plotters are generally not that necessary.

Deciding on the "Little Extras." Another set of questions concerns those little extras—glare reduction screens, antistatic devices, and electrical power surge protectors to name a few. The general answer is that they are important. Those devices that protect the microcomputers are particularly useful. If a facility has clean steady electrical power, the power protection devices are less important but still recommended. Antistatic devices are also recommended. As microcomputers become smaller and more sophisticated, they also become more delicate; static electricity increasingly becomes one of their worst enemies. Thus, it is strongly suggested that all necessary steps be taken to protect the institution's investment. Reduced glare screens, on the other hand, are nice but not essential since the average student will not be spending extensive time with the microcomputers at any one sitting. In summary, it is important to protect your people and your machines, but the degree to which this is necessary is highly dependent on local conditions.

A Quick Look at Maintenance Contracts. Last among the hardware issues covered is the question of maintenance contracts. In general, and in the long run, it is usually less expensive not to purchase such contracts. However, it should be quickly noted that they are very useful in at least two instances. If the annual budget is fixed or tight, maintenance contracts will ensure that the microcomputers can be repaired as needed. While the overall cost may be higher, risk and insecurity are reduced with a maintenance contract. Such contracts may also reduce the burden on the administrative staff. When the computer malfunctions, the staff can simply call in the serviceperson or deliver the machine to the shop according to a prearranged procedure.

Space Requirements

The Microcomputer Lab. Decisions about space "requirements" often result from the mediation of what is needed in order to be comfortable versus what is available. Each microcomputer workstation is comfortable with about five linear feet of space. This allows two feet or so for the machine, another foot and a half for the printer, and an eighteen-inch work space for the student and his or her various manuals, books, and papers. The depth of each station should be about three feet with stations being placed back to back. The space between workstation rows should be about six feet to allow for both seating and circulation. Thus, a school could comfortably put a dozen microcomputer workstations in a room of about 500 square feet having approximate dimensions of twenty feet by twenty-five feet. In other words, in a relatively small room holding ten or twelve workstations, each station requires forty square feet or so. As the room gets larger, circulation economics can be achieved, and the average square feet per workstation could range from thirty-two to thirty-six square feet.

In practice, however, these averages may not be suitable. Many computing facilities, particularly those that have had workstations for terminals tied to mainframe computers, have workstations of six to ten square feet and average workstation sizes including circulation of twenty to thirty square feet. At one institution each workstation is about twelve square feet with an average, including circulation, of about twenty-six square feet. These allocations work but are qualitatively insufficient. Circulation is tight, students must often keep their work papers in their lap, and it is most difficult to have two people at each workstation for demonstration and other instructional purposes.

The Software Library. A second important space besides the microcomputer lab is the software library, which should be easily accessible and easily secured. This room may also be used as the work space for computer facility assistants. The general distribution and sale of computer-related material may occur in this space. While it should be located as closely as possible to the microcomputer lab, its size will depend on the number of functions conducted in the room.

The preferred approach is to use one large room as the micro-computer lab headquarters. This would permit the software library, computer room assistant, paper exchange, and supplies and sales functions to be located in the same space. Such a room would require approximately 100 to 150 square feet for the software library activities and another fifty square feet or so for the storage of computer supplies and spare equipment. The small items for sale, such as floppy disks, could also be stored in this space while the software librarian could be responsible for transactions and the petty-cash box. The three or four computer assistants on duty would require another 200 square feet for desks, chairs, work tables, and so on. The "drop box" function would need an additional 100 square feet. This area would provide for an out-box or perhaps wall racks. It might also hold a chalk or bulletin board and a few chairs and perhaps a table to allow students to organize their work. For other schools and other programs the required dimensions will vary depending on the overall size of the microcomputer program and the number of classes and students to be served.

Time, Space, and Scheduling

Most educators have learned that time is space, that space is time, and that proper scheduling is what converts one to the other. The very same calculus applies to microcomputer programs.

Conventional wisdom holds that it is necessary to have a system for students to schedule machine hours. As the number of software packages increases, this system must accommodate the need for a particular piece of software and a specific machine. It has been found at several institutions that the conventional wisdom may indeed be wrong. Just as continuing education students distribute themselves among the available hours, they seem to distribute themselves among the various computers and among the various software packages. The need to impose an administrative solution does not exist because the suspected problem was found not to exist. There are probably several suggestions in combination that ease the scheduling burden. First, the microcomputer lab should be open during a reasonable number of hours available to adult continuing education students. All computers in the lab should be reasonably well equipped. That is, all computers should be able to run all software packages and support all printer needs. It is most troublesome to have one-third of the computers able to run one-half of the software, another fourth able to run another third, and so on. Students should be permitted to the degree possible to use substitute software, word processors, and spread sheets. Students should also be permitted, indeed encouraged, to do microcomputer lab assignments in the order they prefer. One student may want to start with word processing while another is ready to address data bases. One student may want to do spread sheets while the other finds project managers more useful at a particular time. This is not only good scheduling; it is good education as well. A few prohibitions should also be listed here. As suggested earlier, adult continuing education students can be quite adaptive if the rules of time, space, and scheduling are set and not changed. For example, you should schedule demonstrations early and do not change the date or time. Do not schedule demonstrations in the computer lab without ample preparation. Do not let nonstudent groups use the computers without good reason and ample notice. Be flexible in making assignments and try not to alter the sequence of events once the course gets underway. Trust that adult learners want to learn for powerful personal reasons and that they *will* learn given sufficient flexibility.

James R. Hollowood is involved in educational product development with the Digital Equipment Corporation. He teaches in the Harvard University Extension program and is a consultant to the Arthur D. Little Management Education Institute.

*The use of the microcomputer and video recorder,
combined with traditional lectures, teamwork, case
studies, and exercises, creates a "high-tech/high-touch"
learning experience for adults in management
education.*

High-Tech/High-Touch Management Education

Andrea Warfield

Both management education for adult learners and in-house management training for the administrative staff of Ferris State College (FSC) are being greatly enriched by the use of the microcomputer.

In 1984, FSC became a member of the Thoughtware Network, a consortium of eighteen colleges and universities coordinated by the Higher Education Management Institute (HEMI). Consortium members used Thoughtware computer-based management training modules in continuing education programs to enhance traditional management classes and for internal staff development. As a member of the consortium, FSC received the support and services of HEMI and shared with other educators developmental ideas for the use of the microcomputer and Thoughtware in various areas of management training.

FSC began using the personal computer as a learning tool during the summer term of 1984 in what has come to be called the "high-tech/high-touch" management course. This class, designed for adult learners with little or no management experience, uses the new technology of the microcomputer and video recorder complemented by creative teamwork and highly interactive management exercises to train managers who will work in a "high-tech/high-touch" world.

The elements that comprise this course are: traditional lectures on

B. Heermann (Ed.). *Personal Computers and the Adult Learner.*
New Directions for Continuing Education, no. 29. San Francisco: Jossey-Bass, March 1986.

management theory and concepts; case studies; experiential exercises, such as structured experiences; films; video-recorded participative training exercises produced by learners; and a collection of computer-based instruments produced by Thoughtware called *Assessing Personal Management Skills.*

Course Overview

Early in the course, learners are broken into small groups that are responsible for training the rest of the class on one of the concepts covered in the lectures, text, case studies, films, and exercises. Examples of such concepts are teamwork, the group process, motivation, leadership, training, staffing, performance appraisals, time management, and stress management. One important requirement of the training exercises is that they be completed partially on videotape. Additional requirements on which learners are graded are degree of participation by classroom members, interest to class, creativity, and thoroughness of research.

The Use of Video in Training Exercises. A particularly effective video training exercise, modeled on the paper-and-pencil Antarctica Survival Exercise, was used to demonstrate the group process. This exercise is traditionally completed by having learners pretend they are among ten survivors whose plane has just crashed in Antarctica. They are given a list of ten items that have been salvaged from the plane and are asked individually to rank the items in order of which they think are the most important to keep. They then work in groups to reach a consensus on the rank order of the items. Next, individual and group rankings are compared to a survival expert's rankings, and learners discuss the effectiveness of the group versus the individual rankings of the items.

The video version of this exercise began with the title "Group Decision Making" followed by the names of the training team in block letters. Dramatic background music was played. The next scene was the site of an airplane crash. As the music softened, a voice in the background described the circumstances of the crash. The four students who made up the training team crawled up to the crash site and began talking about what they were going to do. They examined the ten items as they discussed what they should and should not keep, then turned to the class and asked, "What should we do?" The video was stopped at this point, and learners first worked individually, then in groups, to prioritize the items. Both lists were compared to the survival expert's list via actors on the video. Finally, the actors discussed characteristics of effective group interaction, and the video ended with background music.

Because the exercise was very creative, thoroughly researched, of interest to the class, and allowed a high degree of class participation, the group was awarded all the points that could be earned.

The videotaped exercises serve many purposes. One important learning outcome is an awareness of and experience in participative training, a skill of utmost importance to today's managers. Another is the opportunity for trainers to use video equipment and to see themselves on video, a tool that is used increasingly in management training for self-observation and for teleconferences and other forms of communication. The exercises also demonstrate that teamwork and experiential learning can be fun.

Another purpose of the videotaped training exercises is to create a situation in which relatively inexperienced learners must use organizational skills. Learners must work together as a team to plan, create, and rehearse a training exercise. They are then responsible for making the appointment to be taped, getting the script and list of props needed to the media production center, working with the television crew to do the actual taping, and conducting the training exercise in class.

The training exercises are spaced evenly throughout the term (normally one per week over eight weeks) and are presented as the related concepts are covered in class.

The Use of the Microcomputer. Assessing Personal Management Skills, Thoughtware computerized module 1.1, is completed individually by learners based on previous work experience and their behavior in their training teams. The three-hour module is divided into three units, each of which takes approximately one hour to complete: Unit I, "Managing People to Achieve Results," is due one-third of the way through the term; Unit II, "Applying Management Methods," is due two-thirds of the way through the term; and Unit III, "Increasing Your Own Effectiveness," is completed at the end of the term. Since the order of the concepts covered in class and in the training exercises are the same as those assessed by Thoughtware, the learner simultaneously examines each concept, trains or is trained on it, and completes a computerized instrument to examine personal strengths and weaknesses in that area.

An entire class period is devoted to processing each unit on its due date. Therefore, three class periods are used to process the complete module. Students bring their completed student manuals, in which the scores, bar graphs, and charts of module 1.1 are recorded, to class and discuss with their work teams their individual assessments and how these strengths and weaknesses affected task performance in their groups. The sharing of scores is strictly voluntary. No one is forced to disclose information recorded in the student manual.

Kolb's experiential learning cycle is used to process each subunit. This theory contends that a complete learning cycle includes a direct experience, observations and reflections on that experience, abstract conceptualizations based on those reflections, and testing of new concepts in new situations. Learners therefore reflect on a given behavior covered in class and in the training exercises and assessed in the subunit of the Thoughtware module. They discuss how that behavior affected teamwork performance and how these behaviors are important for managerial performance in organizations. Finally, they examine how they will develop strengths in this area for their future careers.

Performance Evaluation. Learner evaluation is based in part on four 100-point tests given throughout the semester. The tests cover theories and concepts dealt with in class and are largely multiple choice, true and false, short definitions, and short essays. Six ten-point quizzes are also given throughout the term. The training exercises are worth thirty points, and the training team is graded as a group; the grading criteria are amount of class participation, interest to class, thoroughness of research, and applicability to subject. Ten points are given for general class participation. Action exercises (part of the Thoughtware module) are collected after each unit is processed, and credit is given for completion.

Benefits of the Course Structure

Combining the video recorder and computerized self-assessment with creative teamwork, lectures, case studies, films, and management exercises results in an extremely rich and multidimensional "high-tech/high-touch" management course. Learners not only examine management theory and engage in highly interactive activities, they also use as learning tools the very technology they will be working with as managers, and they become comfortable with this new technology. With the video, they see themselves as others see them, thus preparing for management as a "performance" art.

The computerized assessment acts as another type of mirror. It enables the learner to assess his or her own strengths and weaknesses privately and to compare these characteristics with managers throughout the country as well as with immediate peers. Thus, creators of Thoughtware have harnessed current computer technology to create a superb tool for expanding human potential and sensitivity. Other business software allows the manager to do tasks more efficiently, thereby enabling him or her to be a more effective manager. Thoughtware focuses directly on this effectiveness by expanding personal introspection, diagnosing management behavior, and offering modules that develop interpersonal skills.

There is a definite contrast between the traditional paper-and-pencil method of filling out instruments in class and completing Thoughtware's *Assessing Personal Management Skills.* Using the traditional method, the instrument is passed out and students are asked to respond to the questions by circling the best answer. The next step is to score the questionnaire, but, since the scoring is usually quite complicated, this step takes at least fifteen minutes, and inevitably some students get lost during the process. Students then compare scores to demonstrate that there are many ways to respond to the same situation, and national statistics are reviewed to show that there are many management styles. Responses to the questionnaire can then be tied to management theory.

Completing Thoughtware's diagnostic series is a completely different experience. The computerized module presents material in a lucid, attractive, and straightforward manner. Interacting with the computer by responding to well-presented material enables the student to participate fully in an esthetically pleasing and vivid learning process.

The scoring is done instantly, and results and comparisons to national norms are shown creatively. Thoughtware's method of breaking down the scores into the various areas of management would be impossible using the paper-and-pencil method of instrumentation because of the time and complicated instructions needed to accomplish this.

Comparison of the learner's scores to national norms through the use of color graphs is much more personal, immediate, and concrete than discussing these norms abstractly in a classroom setting. Finally, a review of the management theory on which the diagnostics are based is interwoven effectively with the questions.

In short, Thoughtware's *Assessing Personal Management Skills* has pushed a contemporary and effective management training method to the state of a totally engaging and absorbing learning experience.

Logistics and Costs of the Course

The technological responsibilities connected with this "high-tech/high-touch" course are fairly light, and the costs low. Since the media production center at FSC is very effectively managed, there have been only minor snags in setting appointments, being videotaped, and returning the tapes to the center.

In order to run the videotaping smoothly, the manager of media production comes to class early in the term to inform learners of their responsibilities and the procedures for getting props, turning in scripts, and making appointments. He prepares them to be videotaped. One week is given for learners to set an appointment sometime during the term to be taped. Learners make their appointment with the course professor, the professor confirms the appointments with the media production manager, and an appointment sheet listing names of team members, training concepts, production dates, props needed, and presentation dates is held by both the professor and the media production manager.

The Thoughtware library is managed by members of the microcomputer lab. The modules in the library are:

1.1: Assessing Personal Management Skills
1.2: Evaluating Organizational Effectiveness
1.3: Understanding Personal Interaction Styles
2.1: Leading Effectively
2.2: Motivating to Achieve Results
2.3: Defining Goals and Objectives
2.4: Improving Employee Performance
2.5: Performance Appraisal

2.6: Managing Time Effectively
2.7: Conducting Successful Meetings
2.8: Managing by Exception
2.9: Stress Management
2.10: Career Planning

The professor demonstrates the only module used for this course, *Assessing Personal Management Skills* early in the class and distributes workbooks to students. Two personal computers with color boards and color monitors are reserved for Thoughtware users, and two DOS disks are left at the lab manager's desk. Students sign the disk out for a maximum of three hours. As with the videotaping, this is an extremely smooth-running operation.

It would be very expensive for a college to write its own computerized diagnostics comparable to those that Thoughtware offers. Thoughtware is extremely cost effective because it is generic: It covers general management areas and can be applied to a wide range of management classes.

FSC's "high-tech/high-touch" management course was so successful that the college's president suggested that a three-day in-house management development retreat for the entire managerial staff of FSC (approximately 108 people) be held during the first week of June 1985. It was his intention at the time that the basis of the retreat would be the completion of Thoughtware 1.1 by all 108 managers, to be accomplished in three groups of thirty-six. However, because of FSC's wiring system, the risk of a technological mishap occurring with thirty-six personal computers being used at one time was too great to allow this. Therefore, the trainers used paper-and-pencil instruments at the retreat and plan to purchase the entire Thoughtware library for ongoing computer-based training. FSC's experience with the paper-and-pencil instruments made both the cost and time effectiveness of Thoughtware apparent.

The cost effectiveness of Thoughtware became obvious when it was noted that the cost of the paper-and-pencil instruments used for the retreat was over $2,000 and the instruments could never be used again. Thoughtware, on the other hand, could be used a countless number of times. The biggest criticism of the retreat was that it took too much time. Much of this time was spent laboriously scoring the complex instruments, which Thoughtware does instantly. For future staff training programs, participants will complete Thoughtware modules individually and privately and then meet for seminars based on each module.

FSC is committed to exploring new technologies for educational use; the use of the microcomputer and video recorder for management education has proved extremely successful. Based on this success, FSC is now launching a management training program for its own staff, and the learning method for this program will certainly be "high-tech/high-touch."

Andrea Warfield, assistant professor of management at Ferris State College, has a background in both sociology and business administration and is a specialist in the behavioral aspects of business management.

*Quality computer-assisted learning materials for the
continuing education of health professionals can be
developed with limited resources. Faculty expertise and
motivation are the keys to success.*

Developing Computer-Assisted Learning Materials for Continuing Education in the Health Professions

Craig L. Scanlan

The marriage of computer technology with the continuing education of health professionals is now more than a decade old. Like many marriages, the relationship was founded upon commonalities in goals and expectations. To those responsible for the delivery of continuing education to health professionals, the computer was viewed as an instructional tool particularly capable of addressing the learning needs of the busy practitioner in a manner fully consistent with the principles of adult education (See, for example, McDonald, 1983; Meadows, 1977; Porter, 1978). This perspective has been strengthened by a growing body of evidence supporting the efficacy of computer-based instructional methods in both undergraduate and continuing health professions education (Breese, Welch, and Schimpfhauser, 1977; Bitzer, 1966; Hoffer and others, 1975). For those involved in the burgeoning field of computer-based instructional design, the relationship represented an ideal opportunity to exploit the full advantages of the computer as an instructional tool (Mulner and Wildberger, 1974).

Inital efforts at "consummating" the marriage employed a main-

B. Heermann (Ed.). *Personal Computers and the Adult Learner.*
New Directions for Continuing Education, no. 29. San Francisco: Jossey-Bass, March 1986.

frame network approach. One such model, the Health Education Network (HEN), was established in 1972 under the auspices of the Lister Hill National Center for Biomedical Communications. Combining the resources of several educational institutions and health care agencies, HEN continues to provide users with access to a wide array of computer-based instructional materials via an on-line subscription service. However, as with other network models, HEN's high subscription costs have generally precluded its widespread use for the continuing education of individual practitioners.

The growing availability of powerful, low-cost micro-processors has shifted the delivery approach from mainframe network systems to personal computers (Schwartz and Hanson, 1982). Within this context, accessibility to hardware resources is becoming less and less a constraint to the use of the computer in continuing education. Indeed, the major barrier now impeding the widespread application of the computer in the continuing education of health professionals is the availability of high-quality computer-based instructional materials. This chapter describes one institution's effort to address this problem.

Background

Stimulated, in part, by a 1984 New Jersey Department of Higher Education grant for acquisition of the necessary hardware, the University of Medicine and Dentistry of New Jersey's School of Health-Related Professions initiated an intensive development plan designed to incorporate computer technology into both its preservice and continuing educational programming. With funding limited solely to capital equipment, the development plan had to be based upon the use of existing personnel resources. The task was made all the more formidable by virtue of the faculty's general lack of experience with computer technology and associated instructional methods. The challenge, therefore, was to mount a broad-based effort to generate quality computer-based instructional materials under conditions of both limited resources and expertise.

Preliminary Considerations

A preliminary review of the literature on the development of computer-based instructional materials provided a sound framework from which to begin. Initially, the advantages and limitations of single-individual versus team production systems were compared (Bork, 1984). Recommendations to the contrary notwithstanding, operational constraints dictated a modified single-individual production system in which faculty would be responsible for both the educational design and technical development of the learning materials.

Based upon the assumption that developing programming expertise among the faculty was neither feasible nor necessarily desirable, a further decision was made to forgo the use of formal programming languages and instead select and employ a CAI authoring language. Based upon cost, ease of use, and technical capabilities, the PILOT language (IBM PC version 1.4) was chosen as the primary authoring system for instructional materials development (Dean, 1978; Schwartz and Hanson, 1982).

A major concern evolving from the literature was that of faculty motivation as a barrier to effective courseware development. With numerous studies (such as Williams, 1977) indicating that faculty resistance was the single greatest deterrent to the diffusion of new instructional technologies in the academic setting, it was clear that the development plan could not succeed without cultivating early enthusiasm for the incorporation of computer technology within the school's educational programming. Maintaining such enthusiasm over what is often a long and arduous developmental process was considered more problematic. Given our budgetary constraints, we found it encouraging that recent research indicated that the primary factors influencing courseware development in the academic setting were not monetary in nature but rather represented the traditional rewards for scholarly life (Hawkins, 1978; Sprecher and Chambers, 1980).

With the relatively small size but complex nature of the school's formal organizational structure (six departments and sixteen program areas), the project's aim to effect broad-based change created additional challenges. A review of the pertinent literature on the diffusion of innovation within organizations (Becker, 1970; Hage and Aiken, 1967; Kaplan, 1967) supported the concept of a decentralized informal leadership approach to the problem.

Of more practical concern were the scheduling problems inherent in organizing any group meeting of a faculty with variable time commitments and frequent off-campus responsibilities. A compounding factor was the assumption that the majority of faculty development time, particularly work sessions using the computers, would occur outside the context of the formally scheduled group sessions. Although not insurmountable, these logistical problems had to be addressed prior to implementing the development plan.

Designing the Instructional Materials

After consideration of the general attributes of the development model, careful attention was given to the process of courseware development and the desired characteristics of the instructional materials that would evolve.

We decided to progress from simple designs to more complex instructional applications. Based upon a common classification scheme of the applications of computer-based learning materials (Meadows, 1977), three levels of development were planned: (1) test and drill applications; (2) interactive tutorials; and (3) simulated management problems. In concept, this sequence would provide the opportunity for early success in courseware development without the necessity of immediately learning all design skills. Within this framework, at each subsequent level of progression, new design capabilities, such as variable feedback to responses and multiple branching, would be developed.

With the goal of the project to develop computer-based instructional materials applicable to *both* preservice and continuing education programming, distinctions between the learning needs and methods appropriate for entry-level health professional students and experienced practitioners (McDonald, 1983) were carefully considered. Since the ultimate goal of professional education, whether preservice or continuing, is to develop and/or refine individuals' capacity to *apply* knowledge to practical ends (in other words, to solve problems), priority was given to developing instructional applications using the simulated management problem format, incorporating design variations specific to their intended use. In regard to preservice educational needs, support for this emphasis on simulated management problems was based upon the common observation that health professional students are seldom given sufficient opportunities within their curricula to apply the knowledge and skills they are developing (Breese, Welch, and Schimpfhauser, 1977; Dugdale, Chandler, and Best, 1982; Gururaj, Akins, and Sewell, 1984).

In regard to continuing education needs, the focus on management problems as an instructional strategy was based upon recent findings that professional competency is "case specific"—that is, that practitioners' capacity to formulate appropriate decisions depends upon sufficiently broad experience and repetitive practice in applying information to the solution of the problems they commonly encounter (Elstein, Schulman, and Sprafka, 1978). Fortunately, good guidance on the design and use of simulated management problems (McGuire, Solomon, and Bashook, 1976) and their computer-based application (Breese, Welch, and Schimpfhauser, 1977; Gururaj, Akins, and Sewell, 1984) already existed.

Clear differences in the nature of learning outcomes characterizing these various levels of application made it apparent that no generic set of design criteria could be developed or applied. Moreover, a review of the extant literature on the evaluation of computer-based instructional materials indicated an overemphasis on technical characteristics, with relatively little attention given to the psychological principles underlying the learning process. In order to address this shortcoming, the development plan incorporated an overview of instructional design principles, emphasizing the application of learning theory to the authoring process (Gagné, Wagner, and Rojas, 1981).

In regard to assessment of the courseware generated by the faculty, the decision was made to emphasize formative, as opposed to summative, evaluation. Formative evaluation represents the *process* of bringing an instructional application to operational readiness (Steinberg, 1984) and consists of several interrelated steps (see Figure 1). Implicit in the process of formative evaluation are significant learning opportunities for the lesson developer. Unanticipated design flaws, "bugs," errors in content, and opportunities for technical enhancement or pedagogical improvement are revealed and provide sound direction for revisions. Ultimately, such feedback assists program developers in refining and expanding their design capabilities according to the needs and expectations of those using the materials.

The Development Plan

Based upon these preliminary considerations, a two-year development plan consisting of three interrelated phases was implemented (Figure 2). Phase I consisted of faculty development. Phase II (in process) addresses instructional applications. Phase III (planned) will focus on dissemination.

The faculty development phase consisted of two stages: (1) the intensive training of a small cadre of selected faculty and (2) the extension of this training of faculty at the departmental and program levels. The intent of the first stage was to develop a small number of highly trained "trainers," capable of sharing their expertise through subsequent decentalized workshop activity at the departmental and program levels. Based upon prior considerations, these initial participants were carefully chosen from among those nominated by their departmental chairs. Selection criteria included departmental support (released time), individual motivation, demonstrated innovativeness, and manifest informal leadership among colleagues. The end-stage goal of this initial intensive training series was the development, by each participant, of a formal plan for the extended training of colleagues in computer-based instructional design at the departmental and program levels.

The second stage of faculty development replicated key elements of the initial training series in a manner consistent with the varying needs and expectations of departmental and program faculty. The intent of this extension stage of development was to expand the base of faculty expertise to include at least one member of each of the school's sixteen program areas. As content experts within their particular fields and with their newly acquired expertise in computer-based instructional design, these individuals serve as key resource personnel within their program areas, providing support for the modified individual production system previously described.

Concurrent with the latter stage of faculty development was initiation of the plan's application phase (in process). The two major stages constituting the application phase are (1) internal software development and (2) commercial software acquisition. Internal software development, based upon the design and evaluative considerations previously described, is employing "model" program formats as the basis for quality instruc-

Figure 1. Computer-based Instructional Materials Formative Evaluation Model

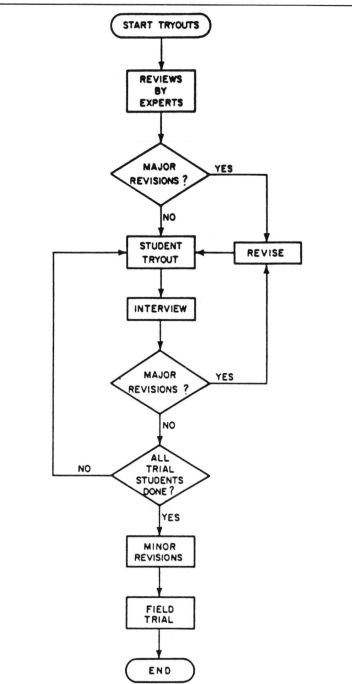

Source: Steinberg, 1984.

Figure 2. Development Plan

Phase	Activities	Timelines

I. Faculty Development	A. Preliminary Tasks
	  1. Designate facility
	  2. Appoint oversight committee
	  3. Acquire initial hardware
	  4. Plan spring workshops
		Fall 1984

	B. Intensive Training Series
	  1. Identify participants
	  2. Acquire materials
	  3. Conduct workshops
	  4. Provide for directed self-instruction
		Spring 1985

	C. Extended Faculty Training
	  1. Acquire additional hardware
	  2. Identify participants
	  3. Conduct training
	  4. Provide for directed self-instruction
		Summer–Fall 1985

II. Application	A. Internal Software Development
	  1. Develop "model" programs
	  2. Field test materials
	  3. Evaluate/refine programs
	  4. Incorporate programs into curricula
		Fall 1985–Spring 1986

	B. Commercial Software Acquisition
	  1. Allocate funds
	  2. Identify available resources
	  3. Develop evaluation criteria
	  4. Initiate preview/
	    purchase mechanism
		Fall 1985–Spring 1986

III. Dissemination	A. Continuing Education
	  1. Plan/implement
	    interdisciplinary conference
	  2. Plan/implement discipline-
	    specific workshops
		Spring–Summer 1986

	B. Establish Resource Center
	  1. Seek/obtain external funding
	    or support
	  2. Designate facility
	  3. Acquire additional resources
	  4. Implement resource center
		Fall 1986–Spring 1987

tional design. The model program formats evolved from the initial intensive training series and, in many cases, provide "template" structures upon which newly trained faculty can build lessons by applying differing content within a semistructured design. In this manner, the advantages of a flexible authoring language (IBM PC PILOT) are combined with the ease of use of an authoring system, without the inherent limitations and constraints characterizing the latter.

Concurrent with the identification, development, and formative evaluation of needed "in-house" instructional materials are ongoing efforts to acquire commercial software applicable to the school's preservice and continuing education needs. Although currently available commercially produced instructional materials for health professionals are limited in number and often of either dubious quality or applicability, their identification, review, and (where justified) purchase were considered an essential and complementary function to the process of internal courseware development. Where quality materials applicable to the school's instructional needs existed, acquisition would, of course, minimize unnecessary duplication of effort. Of perhaps greater importance, however, is the utility of the review process employed with commercially produced software. The application of technical and educational design criteria, developed during Phase I of the plan, is providing important insight into the strengths and weaknesses of these instructional materials and, as a by-product, is sharpening the participating faculty's design assessment skills.

The planned dissemination phase will focus on extending the developed expertise and resources of the school outward to other health-related professional education programs, health care agencies, and individual practitioners. One interdisciplinary conference and several discipline-specific continuing education offerings will provide the initial impetus for dissemination. Ultimately, the intent is to establish a resource center for computer-based instructional materials that will serve the education needs of the state's health-related professions. Besides providing training in educational applications of the computer, the planned resource center will serve as a clearinghouse for instructional materials, thereby achieving the primary goal of increased availability of this important educational medium. Full realization of the resource center concept, however, is contingent upon additional grant funding, which is currenty being sought.

Conclusion

The advent of the personal computer has created new and growing demands for quality instructional materials that can take advantage of the unique attributes of this educational tool. The developmental plan described in this chapter, although still in process, suggests that quality materials can be developed, even with limited resources. The success of such efforts will ultimately depend on the care with which preliminary planning attends to both the principles underlying the design and development of computer-based instructional materials and the unique attributes and capabilities of the instruction(s) and individuals involved.

References

Becker, M. "Sociometric Location and Innovativeness: Reformulation and Extension of the Diffusion Model." *American Sociological Review*, 1970, *35*, 267–282.

Bitzer, M. "Clinical Nursing Instruction Via the PLATO Simulated Laboratory." *Nursing Research*, 1966, *15* (2), 144–150.

Bork, A. "Production Systems for Computer-Based Learning." In D. F. Walker and R. D. Hess (Eds.), *Instructional Software: Principles and Perspectives for Design and Use*. Belmont, Calif.: Wadsworth, 1984.

Breese, M. S., Welch, A. C., and Schimpfhauser, F. "Computer-Simulated Clinical Encounters." *Journal of the American Dietetic Association*, 1977, *70*, 382–384.

Dean, P. M. "Computer-Assisted Instruction Authoring Systems." *Educational Technology*, 1978, *18* (4), 20–23.

Dugdale, A. E., Chandler, D., and Best, G. "Teaching the Management of Medical Emergencies Using an Interactive Computer Terminal." *Medical Education*, 1982, *16*, 27–30.

Elstein, A. S., Schulman, L. S., and Sprafka, S. A. *Medical Problem Solving and Analysis of Clinical Reasoning*. Cambridge, Mass.: Harvard University Press, 1978.

Gagné, R. M., Wagner, W., and Rojas, A. "Planning and Authoring Computer-Assisted Instructional Lessons." *Educational Technology*, 1981, *21* (9), 17–26.

Gururaj, V. J., Akins, Z. S., and Sewell, B. J. "Computer-Assisted Patient Management Simulations in Pediatrics." *Journal of Computer-Based Instruction*, 1984, *11* (4), 117–120.

Hage, J., and Aiken, M. "Program Change and Organizational Properties." *American Journal of Sociology*, 1967, *72*, 503–519.

Hawkins, C. A. "Computer-Based Learning: Why and Where Is It Alive and Well?" *Computers and Education*, 1978, *2* (3), 187–196.

Hoffer, E. P., Mathewson, H. O., Loughrey, A., and Barnett, G. O. "Use of Computer-Aided Instruction in Graduate Nursing Education: A Controlled Trial." *Journal of Emergency Nursing*, 1975, *1* (2), 27–28.

Kaplan, H. B. "Implementation of Program Change in Community Agencies." *Milbank Memorial Fund Quarterly*, 1967, *45* (3), 321–331.

McDonald, C. J. "Computer Technology and Continuing Medical Education: A Scenario for the Future." *Connecticut Medicine*, 1983, *47* (3), 159–162.

McGuire, C. H., Solomon, L. M., and Bashook, P. G. *Construction and Use of Written Simulations*. New York: The Psychological Corporation, 1976.

Meadows, L. S. "Nursing Education in Crisis: A Computer Alternative." *Journal of Nursing Education*, 1977, *16* (5), 13–21.

Mulner, S., and Wildberger, A. M. "How Should Computers Be Used in Learning?" *Journal of Computer-Based Instruction*, 1974, *1* (1), 7–12.

Porter, S. F. "Application of Computer-Assisted Instruction to Continuing Education in Nursing." *Journal of Continuing Education in Nursing*, 1978, *9* (6), 5–9.

Schwartz, M. W., and Hanson, C. W. "Microcomputers and Computer-Based Instruction." *Journal of Medical Education*, 1982, *57*, 303–307.

Sprecher, J. W., and Chambers, J. A. "Computer-Assisted Instruction: Factors Affecting Courseware Development." *Journal of Computer-Based Instruction*, 1980, *7* (2), 47–57.

Steinberg, E. R. *Teaching Computers to Teach*. Hillsdale, N. J.: Lawrence Erlbaum, 1984.

Williams, B. V. "Breaking the Space-Time Barrier: Delivering Continuing Education to the Professional." In P. P. LeBreton (Ed.), *The Assessment and Development of Professionals: Theory and Practice*. Seattle: University of Washington, 1977.

46

Craig L. Scanlan is professor and associate dean at the School of Health-Related Professions, University of Medicine and Dentistry of New Jersey.

The project described here provides ideas that can be used to establish a continuing legal education program using personal computers.

A Model for Practice: Use of Personal Computers for Continuing Legal Education

Sandra A. Ratcliff

The Illinois Institute of Technology (IIT), Chicago-Kent College of Law, opened its Center for Law and Computers in 1983 as the first legal computer education facility of its kind in the country. By establishing a prototype law school computer system, IIT offered a laboratory for students and practicing lawyers to learn to use state-of-the-art tools to improve their productivity. As part of the effort to improve lawyer productivity with personal computers and provide continuing education for lawyers in the Chicago area, Kent College of Law and the Illinois Institute of Continuing Legal Education cosponsored a series of workshops and seminars for lawyers in 1984 and 1985.

This case study reviews the process of establishing the Center for Law and Computers, the continuing education courses for lawyers, and a subsequent project with IBM. Included in the review is a discussion of the operation of the center, an outline and discussion of the continuing education courses, and conclusions drawn regarding the success of the program. A summary suggests implications for planning similar programs.

B. Heermann (Ed.). *Personal Computers and the Adult Learner.*
New Directions for Continuing Education, no. 29. San Francisco: Jossey-Bass, March 1986.

Background of the Project

IIT established the Center for Law and Computers for two purposes. The first was to help solve problems that had emerged as a result of the use of personal computers in the practice of law. Second, the center was to conduct research using computer technology to further continuing legal education.

The research agenda of the center included development of new legal expert systems, a general-purpose legal search language, digital laser disk storage systems, and a digital image communication network. After one successful year of operation, the center agreed to a proposal to conduct a two-year joint study with IBM investigating the effectiveness of using IBM personal computers (PCs) in legal education. The goal of the study was to see how computer hardware and software could enhance the ability of lawyers and law students to learn the law and to use analytical skills that are at the core of legal education.

Continuing Legal Education

When the law and computers project was begun in 1983, an advisory board was formed that consisted of practicing lawyers with an interest in computers. The board suggested a course, "Microcomputers for Lawyers," which was to be taught each semester, one night a week for six weeks.

The course began in 1984, has been taught by practicing lawyers, and has been conducted in the computer lab to provide hands-on experiences. Everything taught relates to the law.

The course is advertised as a course for attorneys who are thinking about purchasing a microcomputer but who are not familiar with the technology and are not sure what to buy. The six two-hour sessions include:

1. The basics:
   - Understanding the parts of a microcomputer
   - Understanding the operating system
   - Understanding microcomputer languages and programs
2. Information management:
   - Using a computer for litigation support
   - Writing reports from data
3. Documents (assembling and revising legal documents)
4. Legal spread sheets:
   - Using Lotus 1-2-3 for litigation
   - Using real estate and tax applications
5. Research:
   - Understanding WESTLAW
   - Understanding LEXIS
   - Conducting fact investigation on NEXIS

6. Communications and the future:
   - Computer networking
   - Contacting mainframe computers through a personal computer
   - Demonstrating new legal expert systems

Lawyers can use the lab evenings and weekends and can have ten free practice hours after the course. After taking the course, many lawyers call the lab for advice on purchases and problems with their personal computers. Since the classes began in 1984, only one student has dropped out. In addition to the IIT courses, numerous workshops and seminars have been presented jointly by IIT with the Illinois Institute for Continuing Legal Education. The seminars have been taught in the laboratory with limited enrollments. Topics have included: programming, selection of a personal computer for a small law firm, office management, and increasing efficiency and profits by using a computer.

Research Project with IBM

In 1984 IBM funded a two-year joint study with IIT to evaluate the use of hardware and software for legal applications. IBM added sixty IBM computers to the Center for Law and Computers in order to support research, including fifteen PC/XTs and fifteen PCs. IBM's "Academic Information Systems Business Unit" was made available to encourage all faculty to use the computers. In additon to installing personal computers, projects were assigned to develop software programs that included a law student briefing/outlining editor, a personal data-base system, an automated document assembly and client interview system, and computer-assisted instruction lessons. To house the additional equipment, a new personal-computer legal lab is to be completed in 1985 that will field-test all these programs.

Successes and Failures

All programs experience successes and failures; this project has been no exception. The center has grown from an operation with twenty personal computers to eighty. The project has been enthusiastically supported by law students at IIT. Students have formed a computer law association, and in two years it has become the largest organization in the school. The Computer Law Association has been working on a new project, and the American Bar Association's Legal Technology Advisory Council is supportive of the group's effort. In addition, the association members are writing articles for newsletters and journals. IIT is now recognized as one of several law schools that provide extensive computer instruction for their students and continuing education for lawyers.

The efforts to provide continuing legal education were well received in 1984 and the six-week courses for lawyers have been well attended. However, several joint seminars by IIT and the Illinois Institute for Continuing Legal Education were canceled due to low enrollments and the cost of operation. Because of the low student-faculty ratio, the courses are expensive to maintain.

Conclusion

In the last two years, IIT Chicago-Kent College of Law has fulfilled its two purposes for its Center for Law and Computers. It has made students aware of problems raised by the emerging computer revolution in law practice and has helped to ease the problems through the computer's integration in the classroom. IIT has also provided continuing legal education in computer usage for Illinois lawyers.

In the future, IIT will continue to provide services for law students and lawyers. In addition, the faculty will conduct new research projects, will publish results of their current projects, and will work actively to solve those problems raised by an emerging computer technology in law practice and legal education.

Sandra A. Ratcliff is assistant director for instructional services at the Illinois Institute for Continuing Legal Education from Northern Illinois University, DeKalb, Illinois, and is past president of the Illinois Adult and Continuing Educators Association.

Management development in a small corporation can be greatly enhanced by computer-based training modules.

Computers for Management Training: The Case Study of a Young, and Rapidly Growing Company

Suzanne Wagner
Susan Heermann

Cernitin America, Incorporated, is a network marketing compny that was founded in 1983 as a distributor of quality health, nutrition, diet, and personal-care products. It began its sales operations with a fifteen-member staff at the 2,000-square-foot corporate office building. In less than two years the staff has grown to sixty, there are tens of thousands of independent distributors spread throughout the United States, and an additional 63,200-square-foot building now houses the warehouse for the eastern half of the country, a distributor training center, and most of the operations offices for the company. Rapid growth is characteristic of a successful network marketing company.

Inability to manage the nearly exponential growth is a common cause of business failure in network marketing companies that start out with the momentum caused by early success. Therefore, one of the most critical administrative keys to long-term success is to have a management

B. Heermann (Ed.). *Personal Computers and the Adult Learner.*
New Directions for Continuing Education, no. 29. San Francisco: Jossey-Bass, March 1986.

staff that is capable of managing effectively in the rapidly changing environment of exceptional growth. Maintaining effective management is an unusually difficult achievement in the context of the frequent changes in organization and day-to-day operational demands caused by rapid growth.

The Need

Cernitin America has been in a continual process of organizational refocusing, redefining roles, and shifting staff to new responsibilities. Staff members who have been with the company since its beginning have assumed many, sometimes unrelated, tasks and often have not severed all previous responsibilities as they have taken on new ones. And staff members have consistently put in countless hours of overtime to ensure organizational success.

Planning a training program had to address these facts. While training was important, the reality of the situation was that it would need to be flexibly scheduled and appropriate to the unusual managerial pressures of the company.

However, since having only sixty employees in the central staff did not justify the hiring of a full-time training director, Cernitin America was faced with the challenge of providing a management development program at low cost and on a piecemeal time schedule. These confounding variables suggested the need for an individualized and highly flexible training program.

Cernitin America was approached by a management consulting firm that specializes in the use of computer-based management training programs. The self-contained, individualized format offered cost advantages compared to alternative delivery systems. Management also began to see beyond the microcomputer's stereotypical word processing and data manipulation functions to its management development capabilities.

The Training Program

The overall goal of the program was to build and unify the management team, getting each manager to look at areas needing development. The structure of the program was developed by the consultant in conjunction with Dr. David Allen (Cernitin America's founder and president) and the staff member assigned the responsibility of management training. The training program was introduced to the staff through a memo from Dr. Allen.

The consultant took responsibility for introducing the software. He was on site for short seminars and individual consultation with key managers, followed by individualized computer-based training. The goal was the development of generic management skills as well as the clarification and alignment of the goals of the company. It was agreed that Cernitin America would send and fund employees with task-specific training needs to specialized seminars (such as one on warehouse management).

The program began with an identified need for formal job descriptions. Because of the history of changing responsibilities, this was an important first step. Without a specific description as a foundation, managers could not evaluate how well a job is being done (what is supposed to be done?) or if the goals are appropriate for the position. And if evaluation is not possible, performance improvement is undirected. Job descriptions were worked out through group and individual meetings among the consultant, each manager, and his/her supervisor.

The next phase of the program focused on setting goals and objectives. Not only improvement but success itself is undirected and left too much to chance if appropriate goals are not set. This phase began with a goals-and-objectives workshop, which included a demonstration of one of the series of computer-based training programs that Cernitin America acquired, a program on "defining goals and objectives." The design of the workshop provided for the familiarization of the staff with the individualized process of computer-based training. It also attempted to heighten the awareness of staff to the importance of setting meaningful goals and objectives, equipping them to begin formulating their own goals in a variety of realms, ranging from problem-solving and creative goals to their own management development goals.

This workshop was followed by work on the computer with a program designed to assess individual manager's skills. It was at this point that managers began to develop familiarity with the computer as a medium for their own understanding and development, particularly as it had to do with increasing their awareness of their managerial strengths and weaknesses. Based on this experience, managers were directed to write management development goals meaningful to them.

Managers were asked to participate in discussions with the consultant related to their own goals and objectives. Worksheets and action plans included in the program's study guide were used in this process, particularly those that supported the writing of measurable, time-specific, results-oriented goals and objectives.

While flexibility was a priority, it was also necessary to create a sense of urgency about completing the computer materials. Periodic seminars with the consultant provided deadlines. Cernitin America supported its managers in scheduling specific times to use programs related to their own developmental needs. While none of the participants has openly expressed reservations about using the computer, there were a few who procrastinated, and unfamiliarity with the medium was felt to be a factor.

The later phases of the training program are individualized, open-ended, and ongoing. Managers use the computer to focus on the particular areas in which they want to improve. While time management is the critical issue for one manager, gaining awareness of interaction styles with employees is the primary need of another manager. Most modules have an action-planning component that guides managers in making connections between what is done at the computer and the day-to-day carrying out of responsibilities.

Completion of the programs will be recorded in employee information files and acknowledged with a memo from the personnel department (the department responsible for management training) and circulated to the manager's supervisor and the company president. With the goal of creating an even greater incentive for employees to complete the computer modules, arrangements were developed with two local colleges to award graduate or undergraduate credit to the participating managers for their work in the management development program if they wished.

The Software

The software used offered a number of general features that contributed significantly to the program. It allowed for action planning, mostly off line on worksheets, so that insights could be shared with supervisors. The software was formatted in an easy-to-use manner and offered "branched" training exercises and problem-solving scenarios, providing feedback on the participants' responses, with the computer prompting alternate solutions.

The management training consultant believes that evaluative feedback is often received more easily in computerized form than when it comes as an assessment from a superior or coworker. For inexperienced staff moving into management positions, the computer-based program is especially valuable in providing performance comparisons with other managers nationally. Comparisons with these national norms helped managers pinpoint particular areas that needed attention but without their risking potential embarrassment.

The following paragraphs describe briefly the computer-based training modules used in this program:

Leading Effectively assesses leadership strategy, based on an on-line questionnaire that is scored automatically by the computer, with the subject privately receiving feedback on his or her style in supervising employees. Employees of the supervisor can also assess the supervisor's skills as part of this program. Assessment of leadership skills are given in eight areas.

Defining Goals and Objectives helps managers focus on developing goals for themselves, for work groups, and for individuals. Distinctions are also made among setting goals for routines, problem-solving, creativity, and professional development.

Managing Time Effectively deals with time management for individual managers and work groups. It assesses the manager's use of time and helps him or her plan improvement in this area.

Managing Stress examines patterns of thinking that led to stress and heightens awareness as to what is stressful for an individual. It also suggests how to plan a program to reduce and cope with stress and help develop a healthy and productive life-style.

Motivating to Achieve Results helps managers evaluate typical work situations, assess their style of handling employee motivation, and develop an action plan to improve motivation.

Improving Employee Performance helps users identify, analyze, and solve performance problems and suggests ways to conduct performance discussions with subordinates.

Conducting Successful Meetings describes elements of successful meetings, provides a look at the way people can hinder or contribute to the success of meeting, and discusses the reasons for calling a meeting. It includes exercises in writing a meeting agenda, simulations to coach skills for keeping meetings on track, and forms for work-group evaluation of a meeting.

Costs

In addition to consultant time for setting up the program and for meeting individually with key managers, the major cost of the program has been an investment of approximately $4,000 in software. In addition to this, there would have been a capital investment of $3,000 to $4,000 had Cernitin America not already owned appropriate hardware. (The software requires an IBM-compatible personal computer with monitor and printer.)

Conclusion

The computerized training program provides Cernitin America with a management training capability that works for the company. It has increased interaction between managers and their supervisors and helped managers to become more focused on producing results that will have a positive impact on performance. Additionally, its flexibility of use accommodates a busy manager's schedule. Finally, the cost is within acceptable bounds for a young company.

Cernitin America plans to intersperse periodic management seminar retreats and seminars attended by individual managers with computer-based training to extend its team-building capacities and to further heighten management performance. The company believes that exposing new managers to uniform and relevant training at the microcomputer is useful for advancing the effectiveness of the corporation and heightening the quality of its services to its clientele.

Suzanne Wagner is vice-president of Cernitin America, Inc.

Susan Heermann is administrative assistant at the Higher Education Management Institute.

Learning contracts allow adult learners to earn
academic credit for off-campus computer activities.

Learning Contracts and the Personal Computer

Harriet W. Cabell

Institutions of higher education face a monumental challenge in attempt-
ing to provide adult learners continuing education in computer usage.
Increasing numbers of adults have school-aged children engaged in computer-assisted learning activities, and they themselves often have personal
computers at home. In many cases they are also involved in a myriad of
computer uses at work. Not only do these adult learners want assistance in
using personal computers but those enrolled in degree programs also want
academic credit for what they already know and what they will learn in
the future.

In colleges and universities there is a rush to expand computer
capability, but a major obstacle is perceived to be the financing of technology. Continuing educators are often unaware of the computer resources
that adult learners have access to in their places of employment. The
opportunity for continuing educators may be less in financing equipment
and more in creatively using and enhancing the computer capability
already available to adults. The possibility of hooking up a personal computer with a worldwide network of electronic communications "empowers
those who learn to use them to make complex judgments in the more
mindful knowledge of alternative futures" (Cleveland, 1985, p. 20).

Business and industry are already far ahead of education in training

B. Heermann (Ed.). *Personal Computers and the Adult Learner.*
New Directions for Continuing Education, no. 29. San Francisco: Jossey-Bass, March 1986.

employees through computer technology. Nor is this gap likely to decrease. Xerox has predicted that by 1990, 80 percent of all Americans will be using new technologies as part of work (Strange, 1984).

At the same time, educators are arguing among themselves about what computer learning should be included in an undergraduate curriculum and under what circumstances academic credit should be allowed. Some are concerned that the high reliance on technology and heavy emphasis on employability may turn out students "with a little stamp on their forehead" showing they are employable rather than educated (Turner, 1984, p. 1).

Within this general context, we must ask ourselves how continuing education can assist individual learners in integrating computer learning accomplished at work or at home into an undergraduate curriculum. How can learning outside of an educational institution be recognized and evaluated? How can issues of academic quality be addressed? How can computer technology be delivered to such a divergent student group? At the same time, how can learners understand the medium as a tool to assist them in the solving of complex societal problems?

The Learning Contract

There is no panacea, but the out-of-class learning contract is an effective educational strategy to assist the learner. The learning contract is the heart of the University of Alabama's New College External Degree Program.

The New College was established in the early 1970s as a separate degree-granting entity of the University of Alabama to provide undergraduates greater flexibility. Former President David Mathews's (1980) strong belief that "the vitality of a university is in its abiding concern for the people it serves" (p. 163) provided an environment to foster the growth of the External Degree Program within the New College. The program is for adults whose educational needs cannot be met through traditional university programs. Guidance is provided each student in determining educational goals, in formulating a total degree program, and in the development of a learning contract.

A learning contract is a written agreement between a student and a faculty member "regarding a particular amount of student work and the institutional reward or credit for the work" (Berte, 1975, p. 3).

Traditional classroom activities cannot possibly provide the flexibility needed by adults who have many opportunities to acquire learning through personal and professional activities. With the learning contract, a student can initiate and design a "course" tailoring learning to meet both individual and institutional goals. Contract learning can be applied to any area of the curriculum and can free a student from the time and space constraints of classroom attendance.

External Degree Program students are located all over the country. The student must complete a minimum of at least one learning contract a year. In its simplest form, the contract answers for the learner: What do I want to know? How will I learn it? Who and what will help me? How will others know I know? When will I complete the learning activity? The faculty member helps the student design the contract, serves as an information resource and colearner, and also monitors and evaluates the experience to protect academic integrity as well as to ensure that the learning has taken place.

In addition to learning contracts, credit for prior learning, previous academic credits, correspondence study, and classroom work can be applied toward the attainment of a degree in the External Degree Program. With the use of the learning contract, students can develop a variety of computer experiences, including the use of the computer, as discussed in Chapter One, as a teaching machine, as a tool to assist in projects, and as a learning resource. The following examples have been altered to conceal the identity of the students and faculty, but they illustrate how computer learning can be facilitated through learning contracts.

Specific Examples

Jean graduated from high school in the mid 1950s, attended a local business school, and became a secretary to the mayor. After marriage, she actively pursued an interest in real estate and became a corporate executive in her husband's highly successful automobile agency. Jean enrolled in the External Degree Program and developed several prior-learning portfolios on the basis of which she received academic credit for art appreciation, real estate sales, and technical writing.

Jean also developed a learning contract with a goal of preparing a paper on southern women in the nineteenth century. While working on the manuscript, she developed a friendship with a faculty member who writes literature for adolescents. The professor encouraged Jean to think of this outlet for publication of her manuscript, "Southern Women." Jean learned of a software package that analyzes manuscripts to determine the readability level for adolescents. She decided to learn the system and gain additional academic credit by means of another learning contract.

To complete this second learning contract, Jean worked both with a faculty member in the reading laboratory and with a creative writing instructor. She set as her goals an understanding and knowledge of how to use a microcomputer, knowledge of a specific software package, and the computation of the readability level of her own manuscripts. To meet these goals, Jean received instruction on the use of the microcomputer, analyzed her own manuscripts and compared them to the reading level of established authors, met with the faculty members regularly, read books and articles, and prepared a short manuscript. At the beginning of the study, Jean said, "I'm scared to death of computers," but, much to her surprise, in three months she accomplished a number of her educational goals: She learned to use the microcomputer; she analyzed all of the manuscripts she had prepared for young readers; and she received academic credit toward her degree. The faculty member reported, "I just acted as a sounding board and helped Jean evaluate her progress. The computer was the real tutor."

Not only individual learners but also groups have enhanced their goals by using the computer as a tutor. For example, a group of five external degree students used a self-paced, interactive management education software course in a pilot study. The module included sohpisticated assessments that compared the students to national norms developed with managers in Fortune 500 companies. Each of the students had five or more years of work experience, and each had expressed an interest in moving into a higher management position. Each student reviewed the software and answered a series of questions as part of a faculty-designed learning contract.

Course content and comprehension of management principles were rated highly by all of the students. However, as a result of using the management education software, no student developed an individual learning project from the experience, and none reported a change or confirmation of his own personal management style; which was one of the goals stated by the pilot group. The faculty member evaluating the project reported, "Perhaps I violated the first rule of contract development as I didn't encourage the students to define individual goals for using the software. I'm afraid it ended up as just a review of the software."

A second phase in the use of interactive software is planned, based on findings from the pilot group. Apparently, without the students' initiative in goal setting, even interactive material reinforces passive learning, and students will not necessarily be engaged in the project if everything has been predetermined by someone else. "The focus needs to be on the student's decision to want to learn, what to learn, and how to learn it" (Hodgkinson, 1975, p. 83).

Some continuing education students are already computer technicians and have extensive knowledge of computer languages such as Fortran, COBOL, Pascal, and BASIC. These languages are no mystery, and attempts to enforce university course requirements by repeating such learning are considered a waste of precious time. The practice of awarding credit for prior learning allows the student's knowledge to be verified, and the learning contract individualizes new learning based on already acquired knowledge.

Foster is just such a student. He entered the External Degree program as a senior piping designer for Olin Chemical Corporation. Frequent trips to construction sites made traditional coursework impossible. Years ago, Foster left engineering school to be married. His letter to his adviser illustrates the evolution of his computer competence gained experientially.

> Computer programming is my first love and occupies all my time at work since I am a programmer/systems analyst. It occupies most of my time since I do contract programming for several clients as well as specifying and setting up business computer systems. In my spare time I have managed to write programs to analyze mortgages, amortize loans, calculate APR, size pumps and calculate pipe flow losses, calculate heat transfer in heat exchangers, analyze electrical networks (using complex number inverse matrix), perform stress analysis on structural networks, and maintain records for project files for the design group at Olin. . . .
>
> I have specified, ordered set up, and placed into operation a multiuser computer system here at Olin to do our daily records maintenance, drawing-file organization, and build a data base of all our project files (there are thousands). This system allows for electronic mail, word processing, spread-sheet analysis, and other custom programs to operate under a multiuser multitasking environment for as many as eight terminals. . . . Also, my partner and I have gone into the computer consulting business and are currently working on a large data-base type system for the local sheriff's department. . . . If you have a number for the computer down there, I could communicate with you using that method.

After much thinking and discussing of how to integrate and add to this vast amount of computer knowledge and experience, the faculty adviser and Foster decided on a three-semester-hour learning contract entitled, "Z80 Assembler Language Programming." In fulfilling the goals of the contract, Foster is putting together documentation on data input, checking for frequency of error for potential users, and writing instructions for each program. In addition to regular discussion with the project director, Foster is submitting a total of ten small-to-medium-sized assembly programs for review and suggestions. The final evidence of learning is a large program noting the techniques needed to develop the system.

Without the learning contract, students such as Foster might be bored in traditional computer classes and unable to prepare themselves for an environment that places a high premium on creativity, problem solving, and integrative thought.

Contracts can also facilitate the ability of students to use the computer as an educational tool. For example, Robert's parents insisted that he enter college immediately after high school in 1952. Two dreadful years of C's, D's, and F's ended formal schooling. Thirty years later, he had become a very successful businessman, father of four daughters, an avid reader, pilot, ham radio operator, and senior warden of his church. In the midst of his highly active life-style, Robert suffered a massive heart attack. The enforced leisure turned Robert toward continuing his education. He received prior-learning credit for his pilot's license, his amateur radio operator work, real estate sales, and his extensive management and marketing knowledge.

A number of continuing education courses interested Robert. By using the learning contract format, Robert added additional resources to the learning experience and planned an evaluation with the help of a faculty director. In essence, Robert developed a survey course, "Introduction to Microcomputers, BASIC." After the first computer experience, Robert became "hooked" and utilized an additional short methodology contract, "Introduction to Lotus 1-2-3." Robert planned to use this spreadsheet expertise in a small gold business he operated, but he sold the business because of health problems. "Oh, well, all the banks and businesses use them," he said. "It keeps me current."

This example illustrates how effective and educationally sound the contract is. Robert was able to utilize a noncredit continuing education resource for academic credit while continuing his learning at his own pace. Robert also enthusiastically explored several humanities courses and enrolled in an intensive summer seminar in the social sciences area. His papers were constantly corrected, revised, and made final on the personal computer that he purchased after his contract learning. He carries his personal computer everywhere—in the car, to work, and to meetings—and at night he transfers his written notes onto his microcomputer.

With the assistance of the personal computer, Robert's transformation into a superior writer is exciting for him as well as for his faculty mentors. His grades are now all A's and B's. He is presently working on a contract entitled, "Installation and Operation of an Electronic Bulletin Board." The contract utilizes his own initiative and "need-to-know." Upon completion of this contract, Robert will have used the contract format in order to learn the use of new technology for writing, for developing spread sheets, and for communication. Best of all, he has become an avid participant in the computer learning environment.

Figures 1 and 2 show a portion of a learning contract. They illustrate how the learning contract may be used to encourage the adult learner to integrate curricular and extracurricular activities.

Conclusion

Contract learning is not a solution for all of the problems of computer education, but it does reduce ambiguity for both the student and the faculty member because it requires specific educational goals, methods,

Figure 1.

5. GOALS AND OBJECTIVES

What further learning do you propose for this experience? What knowledge, understanding, skill, attitude, or value is sought?

Student Proposal:

1. To learn to adapt and modify an electronic bulletin board program for use in the New College External Degree Program.

2. To demonstrate the value of a BBS and electronic mail service.

3. To tailor the program for simple use by EXD students and faculty.

4. To learn how to provide compatability among types of equipment.

5. To learn cost factors for providing BBS service to EXD.

6. To learn to adapt and modify the program to allow students and faculty to execute contracts, receive, reply to, and send mail. Also to store (download) files, retrieve (upload) files.

6. METHODOLOGY

How do you propose to acquire this learning? What tasks, projects, experiences, exercises will you do? How will you use the **RESOURCES (7◊)?**

Student Proposal:

1. To adapt an existing Basic language program by rewriting and modifying it to make it appropriate for EXD work.

2. To add program lines that will make the program easier to understand for the "noncomputer" user (user friendly).

3. To instruct interested persons in the EXD program in the use of the BBS.

Faculty (Project Director) Comments

Steps should be taken to limit the users to EXD students and their Project Directors. Bulletin boards must be examined very closely to be certain that the security is adequate to protect the system from unauthorized users.

Faculty (Project Director) Comments

The programmer must also take into account the almost endless possibilities for user error and misinterpretation of input allowed by the program.
After Step #1, student needs to contact me before proceeding further.

Figure 2.

---

7. RESOURCES

Who are the people who can help? What places and things will be of assistance? Please supply the proposed bibliography that will be used.

Student Proposal:

C. E. Bowen, "Building a BBS," 80 Micro, May 1984-May 1985.

J. R. Brown, Instant Basic, Prentice-Hall, 1980.

William Barden, What do you do after you plug it in? Wiley Publishers, 1982.

TRS-80 Operation and Basic Language Reference Manual, TRS Publications, 1983.

TRS-80 Mod III Disk System Owners Manual, TRS Publications, 1983.

Extensive use of a TRS-80 Mod IV and a TRS-80 Mod 100 interface with a modem and a printer.

Consultation with local experts in the field of electronic communications.

Related books, magazines, and articles from home library.

Additional bibliography to be developed as project progresses.

8. EVALUATION

What evidence will you show to demonstrate the learning? (Some options are listed on the back page, 10)

Student Proposal:

A hands-on presentation and demonstration utilizing a TRS-80 Mod IV, modem and printer.

Demonstration will include:
1. Using the system.
2. Accessing the BBS.
3. Reading bulletin and mail.
4. Leaving bulletins and mail.
5. Downloading files.
6. Uploading files.
7. Changing system defaults.
8. Security devices.
9. Student will provide analysis of compatability factors and costs.

The system will be set up at the EXD office and will be accessed by a computer from another location.

The system will contain files that will give a brief description of the system, how it works and how it was developed. Hard copy can be obtained from these files as well as all files in the BBS.

3	Semester hours credit are proposed for this experience.
120++	Approximate time in total hours (e.g. 120 hours total is the guideline for a 3 Semester hour experience).
	Check here if experience is to be pass/fail. (Student must complete the P/F form at registration)

Faculty (Project Director) Comments

Assistance can also be gained from users of the system. Paying attention to their comments and observing their operation and access to the system.

Faculty (Project Director) Comments

(What are the arrangements for evaluation?)

I will need several hours of access to this system to evaluate it. It is preferred that the student dedicate a Saturday to come to Birmingham with his equipment and software for my evaluation.

and evaluation techniques. The contract also allows the student to develop new skills based on individual motivation, curiosity, creativity, and willingness to experiment, building on the skills and abilities as well as the needs of the learner.

Faculty members who facilitated contracts in the computer area reflect a positive attitude toward their experiences. One commented, "I like it because it lets me know what's going on out there. It also makes these students in tune with the real world. They know the general database application, word processing, and spread-sheet application. The biggest problem for me is access to the demonstration of the student's knowledge. One student had to rent a computer, and I had to go to his house to see it, but we got the job done."

The positive reactions of both faculty and students in the External Degree Program underscore the desirability for institutions to explore the use of the learning contract to facilitate computer learning. It is virtually impossible to prepackage educational experiences in the use of the computer that will meet all the varying needs of the adult learner. The use of the learning contract is a promising way of achieving this end.

References

Berte, N. (Ed.). *Individualizing Education by Learning Contracts.* New Directions for Higher Education, no. 10. San Francisco: Jossey-Bass, 1975.

Cleveland, H. "Educating for the Information Society." *Change,* July/August 1985, pp. 13–21.

Hodgkinson, H. L. "Evaluating Individualized Learning." In N. R. Berte (Ed.), *Individualizing Education by Learning Contracts.* New Directions for Higher Education, no. 10. San Francisco: Jossey-Bass, 1975.

Mathews, D. C. *A Mansion's Memories.* Huntsville, Ala.: Strode, 1980.

Strange, J. "Technology and Education; Some Strange Thoughts." Unpublished manuscript, 1984, pp. 1–29.

Turner, J. A. "New Computer-Science Accrediting Plan Is Assailed by Liberal Arts Educators." *Chronicle of Higher Education,* 1984, *28* (16), p. 1.

Harriet W. Cabell is associate dean of adult education of New College, the University of Alabama, and is director of the External Degree Program. She has served as chair of the board of the Council for the Advancement of Experiential Learning (CAEL) and has been a consultant to numerous programs for adult learners.

The personal computer has a wide variety of practical uses for the course developer, instructor, and educational manager that can not only simplify day-to-day activities but also improve the quality of educational programs.

The Personal Computer as a Vehicle for Learning in the Workplace

John E. Thomasson
Ronald E. Larsen

The usefulness of the personal computer in education has been a common topic in both educational and technical publications for some years. However, as Chapter One indicates, the bulk of the literature seems to deal with only one general topic—computer-assisted instruction (CAI), or the use of the PC as an electronic teacher. Of course CAI is an exciting area, but the PC has other practical uses for traditional teachers, course developers, evaluators, and administrators. Indeed, the push to use microcomputers in education is probably not due so much to the excitement and variety they add to learning as to their simple practicality. They ease the day-to-day burdens of educators.

The labor-saving and cost-saving characteristics of the PC account for its extensive use in industry—particularly in electronic data processing companies like NCR Corporation. NCR provides an excellent example of an organization testing the limits of the educational uses of personal computers. In the first place, the company is one of the leaders in the computer industry, which means that the NCR education function can take advan-

B. Heermann (Ed.). *Personal Computers and the Adult Learner.*
New Directions for Continuing Education, no. 29. San Francisco: Jossey-Bass, March 1986.

tage of both the equipment and the expertise that represent the latest developments in computer technology. Secondly, in the workplace of the 1980s, continuing education is more than a social or moral issue. It is a business necessity that NCR has resolved to meet. The company annually provides over half a million student days of education to over 115,000 participants around the world. This is a significant investment in human capital, and NCR has found it possible to optimize that investment by rigorously applying new technologies in its educational activities. This combination of technological expertise and a mature educational organization has made NCR and similar companies the proving ground for the educational uses of personal computers.

The Personal Computer as Teacher

At NCR, as elsewhere, computer-assisted instruction is the most familiar educational use of the personal computer. In CAI, the computer is programmed to (1) present information on the screen, (2) pose questions or problems to the student, ((3) accept answers, and (4) immediately provide an appropriate feedback message—either confirmation of the student's correct answer or remedial instruction. Today's personal computer allows a wide variety of presentation methods; text, graphics, animation, and audio can add to the clarity of messages. The student typically responds by using the keyboard, although other response modes, such as touch screen, joystick, or wand sensors, can be used depending on the capabilities of the personal computer and the instructional design of the course.

The speed and memory capacity of the PC is now adequate to respond to each student's unique needs in a constant interactive process. This results in a high level of individualization of instruction, with each student receiving precisely the information he or she needs at the right time and with the appropriate level of detail. Both the effectiveness and the efficiency of instruction are enhanced.

An example of an effective use of CAI in technical training at NCR is a course designed to teach software developers how to use a set of productivity tools called collectively the *Software Development Environment.* These are computer programs that run on a large mainframe computer and do for the programmer what a word processor will do for a writer. To learn to use the tools, personal computers use a CAI course on their PCs. The course first introduces the function and capability of each tool and then provides practice by exactly simulating the way each tool would be used on the mainframe computer. Programmers report having no difficulty moving from the PC simulation to use of the tools on the large computer. Moreover, since they can choose which lessons they want to study, they can learn each tool when they have a need to use it. Without the CAI course on the PC, programmers would be only partially productive while waiting for a scheduled classroom course; they would then learn all the tools at once and might forget those that were not put to use soon after the class.

Similar examples of CAI for technical training at NCR are abundant. One CAI course teaches how to program using the BASIC language. Students are introduced to language instructions and techniques and have an opportunity to practice new skills by programming on the same PC that serves as their private tutor.

Another CAI course teaches the principles of diagnosing and repairing a computer printer and has built-in exercises in which the student performs adjustments on the equipment being studied. The CAI course can be completed on an average of five hours, and students attain competence levels equal to those who spend twelve hours using a self-instruction workbook.

Another successful series of CAI courses teaches personal-computer skills on the PC itself. Students are introduced to the keyboard and controls, and operating software, and application programs such as word processing and spread sheets. Some of these courses, generally those that teach basic skills or skills that are relatively common across different hardware and applications, are purchased from outside publishers, while others that teach information and skills unique to NCR's hardware or procedures are developed internally.

At NCR, most of the nontechnical skills taught through CAI concern management development. The company was using an extensive simulation to teach international business management skills as early as the 1950s, and the process was computerized in 1971. The program lasted a few more years but was eventually abandoned because of its limited target population and the burden of using cards for data input on a mainframe computer.

Computerized management training in the company was then neglected for some time. Only in the last two years has the availability of PCs and affordable software made it practical to offer CAI management training on a broad scale. NCR has now developed PC training programs on time management, English grammar, speed reading exercises, and a labor negotiation simulation. Off-the-shelf packages include the courses in speed reading, financial management, basic management principles, and project management. The curriculum is further enhanced by the availability of tutorial segments accompanying management applications available on the PC. For example, software designed to help a manager analyze financial statements or make business decisions will include extensive tutorials to teach novice managers the basics of finance. These tutorials are typically of high quality and are essential to the user of the program. Yet they are seldom treated in the literature as educational tools.

In many ways, management training topics test the limits of CAI. The essence of management is getting things done through other people. Therefore, interpersonal skills, with their infinite variations, are still most effectively taught through more traditional methods. However, the computer can be used to great advantage in drill-and-practice sessions to teach basic knowledge or to simulate the financial effects of business decisions.

The PC can also be used to present simulations. An example concerns the Software Problem/Enhancement Control System (SPECS), a central computer system used for product improvement and quality assurance. To learn how to use SPECS, students use a PC programmed to simulate the interactions that a software analyst has with the mainframe computer. Narrative explanations and directions are superimposed on the screen to lead the learner through typical interactions. In this way, students gradually gain information and practice until mastery is reached. Upon completing the CAI simulation, students can access SPECS just as they learned on their PC. The simulation on the personal computer develops competence, instills confidence, and provides another extremely important benefit: Critical data stored in the files of the mainframe computer are protected from inexperienced students who might make mistakes that could create serious problems in the actual computer files.

The Personal Computer as a Course Development Tool

Every course developer at NCR is required to design and prepare educational packages that best meet previously established training needs—whether the material is for standard classroom-based instruction, traditional self-instruction, or CAI. Such development means writing, and the personal computer's word processing software has become almost indispensable for writers. Student and instructor manuals are composed, edited, updated, and refined with remarkable ease when the course developer takes advantage of word processing on a PC. NCR course developers also extend this efficiency to the preparation of required status reports and design documents that are integral parts of the quality assurance function in NCR's standard course development process. Many of the required reports are stored on disk in skeleton format so that the course developer need only "fill in the blanks" on the screen of the PC. Timely and accurate information about course development projects is thus made easily available to all who need it.

Instructors have found the word processor to be an advantage as well. Each student in an NCR course is evaluated against objectives set for the course. Often a narrative report is provided to the student and/or the student's manager. Many NCR instructors employ their PC and word processing software to speed the creation of student evaluations and make them more informative. Common comments that appear on evaluation reports are stored on a disk so that the instructor can prepare a thorough and individualized evaluation of each student by assembling and customizing prewritten comments. This "writing by paragraph," supplemented with any comments unique to an individual student, has greatly enhanced the value and acceptance of evaluations.

Still another application of personal computers in the course development process is exemplified by an NCR education department that has linked its personal computers together in a network. At the Central Technical Education Center, near Dayton, Ohio the the course developers working on CAI and interactive videodisk development are assigned to project teams with each individual having a particular specialty. The instructional designer will use a PC to enter course specifications, extract essential information, and enter scripts and other information into the central file. The programmer will access information relevant to his or her needs and add additional information into the system. The project manager, by using a PC, can monitor the status of the project, generate and update both schedules and assignments, and can ensure that all activities are coordinated. Each team member, therefore, has precisely the information needed. Any changes and updates are available as soon as they occur; no one need worry about working with an out-of-date draft. The person preparing manuals for a course can access the script prepared by the video producer so that correspondence between each course component is assured. Significantly, very little paperwork is generated until the project is nearly complete and printed copies are required for production. Design documents, drafts, status reports, and final versions are all prepared by team members on their personal computers, stored on disk, and are available to others in the network. Software even handles the formerly time-consuming operation of creating and updating flowcharts, which are essential to the development of interactive video instruction.

Instructional designers working on CAI, of course, find the personal computer indispensable. Whether using a general-purpose programming language like BASIC, a specialized CAI programming language like PILOT, or one of the menu-driven CAI authoring systems, the NCR course developer can create, test, modify, and update a CAI course on the personal computer.

The Personal Computer as an Aid in Producing Visuals

A teacher's competence is a function not only of subject matter expertise but also of the impact with which he or she can deliver the material. One of the best tools for enhancing that impact is the appropriate use of visual aids, which give form to objects or concepts that could never be described adequately through simple oral explanation. The PC, once again, can be used as a tool by educators in the production of these valuable instructional aids.

NCR uses the PC in a number of ways to produce visuals. For example, any graphics enhancement of traditional CAI can be considered a visual aid. In its simplest form, this concerns changing colors, underscoring, or zooming to highlight the critical points in presented text. In more advanced CAI, a course developer can create graphs to represent data, or even have the PC draw pictures to give shape to a concept. Finally, computer animation gives movement to screen graphics. At present, the use of animation is limited because of the difficult programming involved in its production—a single line drawing of a finger pressing a button might take several hours for a programmer to produce. However, advances in equipment, such as digitizing cameras and the development of libraries of animation programs will make animation much more common in the future.

Useful aids for traditional classroom courses can also be produced with a personal computer. At NCR, course developers can create hard copies of screen graphics by using dot-matrix printers. To show graphics to groups, instructors can either project the image from a PC screen directly to a larger screen, or, for better resolution, they can produce overhead transparencies on a six-pen plotter. A typical plotter will quickly draw a color image directly on an overhead slide. Using this kind of equipment, a course developer with no special artistic ability can create text slides, in various colors and type fonts, at a rate of about five to ten per hour.

A personal computer is also used at NCR to help produce high-quality thirty-five-millimeter slides. About fifteen years ago, the creation of presentation slides was a difficult and expensive process. Text was produced with rub-on letters, and artwork was done manually. When a paste-up was completed, it had to be sent to a professional to photograph and develop into the finished slide. Only one text slide (with no artwork), could be laid out per hour, and it would take about three days to send, photograph, develop, and receive the finished slide. Obviously, the expense involved in this kind of production allowed slides to be used for only the most important presentations.

Now, however, a computer-aided process has greatly simplified the procedure. Text is entered on a PC. The size is set, the text is positioned, the colors are chosen, and some graphics may be added. If additional artwork is required, the data are transmitted to a computerized design station, at which an artist creates drawings on the slide, sets fonts, and adds borders and other enhancements. The finished design is stored on an eight-inch floppy computer disk, which is taken to a film recorder in an adjacent room. The film recorder produces thirty-five-millimeter slides from the data stored on the disk.

There are many advantages to this system. Up to thirty text slides or four to five art slides can be produced per hour, which results in a cost savings of about 50 percent when compared to alternative processes. Qualitative enhancements are as important as the cost savings. The quality of the slides is now more consistent, since pencil-to-paper artwork has been eliminated. Additionally, many creative tools are now available to the artist. Zooming, shadows, repetition, reverse images, and other special effects that would take hours to draw are now possible practically with the push of a button. Charts may be generated instantaneously. Pictures may be simulated electronically. Colors may be changed. Shapes may be changed or moved easily. Once created, images may be stored and reused.

The entire process constitutes a revolutionary change in the production of presentation visuals. Turnaround time is now less than a day. The PC is only a part of the equipment used, but its flexibility makes it the ideal device to begin the process.

The Personal Computer as a Communications Tool

Personal computers become powerful aids to the educator when they are linked by telecommunication lines or networks. For example, the PC screen can display charts, diagrams, and graphics to students who are participating in teletraining hundreds or thousands of miles away. Interactive audio teletraining with an instructor teaching students in two or more remote locations can be effective by itself, but with the addition of high-quality visuals at each location, interest, acceptance, and learning are substantially enhanced. The teletraining instructor can prepare visuals on a PC and store them on disk for later use during the teletraining session. The visuals can then be transmitted over standard telecommunication lines to the personal computers at the remote sites. Relatively simple visuals can be sent during the teletraining session, and they will appear on the students' PC screens almost immediately to illustrate the instructor's point. More complex graphics and visuals, however, are best sent in advance of the teletraining and stored on disk in the students' PCs. The instructor merely transmits a command to the students' PCs to transfer the required visual from disk to screen, which is much faster than transmitting a complex graphic image over telecommunication lines. A significant feature of this system is the ability of any site (instructor or student location) to add comments, to highlight with arrows or underlines, or to draw superimposed images on the PC screens at all participating sites. Adding visual interaction to the verbal dialogue with students significantly improves learning.

The variety and quality of images that can be sent from one PC to another over telecommunication lines is constantly improving. NCR is now evaluating, for example, a product that will digitize a video image (convert a still image from video tape, disk, or camera to a form that can be stored on the magnetic disk of the PC). This will allow any video image to be transmitted from the instructor's PC to the students' PCs in a teletraining session.

Students in NCR classes may also use their personal computers (equipped with proper software and telecommunication modems) to send electronic messages to their remote instructor or to distant student peers. Recently, for example, a series of lectures on data-base design was telecast by the National Technological University (NTU) with NCR joining other locations in the country receiving the satellite signal. Students used personal computers to send questions by electronic mail to the professor, who then answered them during the next day's telecast.

Telecommunicating with the personal computer is also useful to

NCR's widely distributed education centers, which regularly exchange information on budgets, class and student scheduling, activity reports, and updates to student and instructor manuals. Telecommunication of data files between personal computers is a less expensive and far more timely way to manage information than through regular mail.

Another valuable way to combine personal computers and telecommunication is to access the many on-line data-bases of educational information that are available at nominal or no cost to educators. Of the 2,500 data bases available on more than 350 on-line services, many are of particular value to the educator. One of the larger on-line services, CompuServe, offers access to Grolier's Academic American Encyclopedia, information from the Association for Development of CAI, the Educational Products Information Exchange, Educational Research findings, a general forum for education professionals, news from the College Press Service, and a means for taking or creating CAI courses. NCR educators use their PCs to find valuable information in many of these resources.

A PC can also communicate with a CAI program on a mainframe computer. Unlike a terminal, however, the PC permits lessons to be "downloaded"—that is, transmitted to the memory of the PC—so that the student may study at his or her own pace without costly communication-line charges. The student's performance in the course and certification of completion can be "uploaded"—transmitted back to the mainframe computer—in a second telecommunication connection. In a variation of this procedure, students at NCR use their PCs to receive a test covering material in conventional self-instruction courses. Each student's test consists of questions randomly drawn from a bank of questions in the central computer. The PC receives the set of questions, presents them to the student, and stores the student's answers, which are then uploaded to the central computer. A passing grade results in automatic recording of successful course completion and, when appropriate, the student's eligibility to attend a classroom-based course.

The Personal Computer as a Controller for Other Devices

The personal computer is also useful in controlling other instructional devices. It can, for example, control multiple projectors—motion and still—for large group presentations. For individualized presentations, it is unmatched for controlling the laser videodisk. Interactive videodisk instruction (IVI) can present any one of 54,000 still images or full motion sequences with accompanying monaural or stereo sound. Combined with the features of CAI, IVI permits the educator to individualize and enhance the interest, clarity, and effectiveness of an instructional presentation. Some systems present computer-generated displays on the screen of the PC and images from the videodisk on a separate video monitor while others, such as the NCR InteracTV, use the PC screen to display both video and superimposed computer-generated information.

One NCR course combining the PC with the videodisk is designed for bank tellers. Motion with sound is used to introduce topics and to show such important skills as proper currency counting procedures. When motion is not required, as in learning to recognize counterfeit money or decide whether a check can be cashed, still images from the videodisk are displayed. The visual images add several important dimensions to the teller's training. Watching and hearing a customer transaction, for example, is far more effective than reading about it. A video image of a check is far more realistic than one simulated with computer graphics. Confirmation or corrective feedback is far more meaningful when the message is superimposed on critical visual elements seen in the problem situation or question. The IVI teller training course also maintains a record of student progress, which is available to the student on demand and is used by the PC to help determine appropriate presentation and testing strategies for individual students.

The Personal Computer and Management Education

Education, like any other enterprise, does not run itself. Supplies and flows of various resources must be managed to assure that organizational goals are met as efficiently as possible. Large computers have been used for many years to provide the information necessary to facilitate resource management in education, but only recently have personal computers acquired the power necessary to function as management information tools.

NCR uses PC spread-sheets applications to meet several of the information management needs associated with its educational activities. A spread-sheet, essentially an electronic facsimile of an accountant's worksheet, is used to maintain the budget for NCR's main educational facility in Dayton, Ohio. The facility, known as Sugar Camp, is as large and active as a small college, with the capacity to provide about 200,000 student days of education annually. Because the education groups that use Sugar Camp maintain their own budgets, the budget for the facility contains few of the instructor's salaries or other direct educational expenses. However, capital and maintenance expenditures are substantial, and the PC is a valuable tool for recording and processing the data necessary for facilities administration.

Spread sheets can also be used to track student progress and to administer instruction itself. For example, a PC is used by NCR's sales education group to track over 700 students in thirty groups moving through thirty separate curricula. These curricula include time in Sugar Camp and in remote sales offices. About 200 separate spread sheets are maintained to control the scheduling of housing for students, classroom space, instructors, courses, and equipment. These spread sheets are consolidated periodically into a summary report. Then an extract for each group of students is produced to isolate conflicts with equipment or instructors, followed by an extract for each of the three major sales divisions to isolate conflicting demands for classroom space. This kind of application pushes the limits of a PC, as evidenced by the large 512-kilobyte random access memory and ten-megabyte hard disk required for the process. However, the system works quite well with these enhancements, and the various spread sheets are maintained by nontechnical, administrative support people.

Data-base management applications are used to manage certain self-instruction and evening courses for NCR employees. Whereas electronic spread sheets are like accountants' worksheets, data bases are somewhat like filing cabinets. They keep lists of data, or files, in orderly arrangements so that they can be accessed quickly or printed into meaningful reports. An example of a data-base management application using a PC can be found at the NCR Management College, the corporate management training group at NCR. To aid the NCR Management College in managing the self-instruction courses it offers employees, NCR maintains the records of enrollment, test completion, and course completion on a personal computer. Since the system allows the data to be sorted, reports can be made by organization, by date of completion, alphabetically by student, or by any of the other items in the student's record. This greatly simplifies the process of billing, issuing certificates, and reporting to management.

Naturally the processing power and storage capacity of a micro-computer is quite limited when compared to the larger minis or main-frames. Yet, the PC can play an important role in fully automated computer-managed instruction. Such a system is currently under development at NCR's Central Technical Education Center (CTEC). At CTEC's self-paced learning center, each student will log on to the computer management system mainframe by using a PC as a dumb terminal (a terminal having no processor of its own). The student will then use various self-instruction devices, including the same PC that he or she logged on with, and then take criterion tests on the PC. The tests will be scored automatically and the results will be stored in the memory of the central mainframe. In the last phase of implementation, a course monitor may observe the progress of any student simply by tying into the system network.

The object of this type of system is to keep up-to-the-minute records of students' qualifications, so that only field engineers qualified to work on designated equipment will be called upon to do so. So far, the first phase of the plan has been completed. The PCs are currently used for content presentation, scheduling, testing, and storing the results of the tests. Subsequent phases of development are now under way, and the system promises substantial economic returns.

The experience of CTEC shows that self-paced, programmed learning allows field engineers to complete their programs 30 to 50 percent faster than through traditional classroom instruction, and they report that the quality of learning is better. Furthermore, when the complete computer-managed instruction system is in place, the clerical tasks of human administration of many courses will be almost entirely circumvented. Students themselves will sign on to the system, and the system will track them until they complete the course. At that time, their education records will be automatically updated. All together, the net return on investment for the system is projected to be between 40 and 50 percent over four years.

The Personal Computer and Other Aspects of Employee Development

A significant difference between NCR and traditional colleges or universities has to do with the ultimate goal of the education provided. At NCR, education is not an end in itself. It is one of many opportunities for employee development offered by the company, and it is provided in the trust that the development will make employees more effective or productive in their work.

With this in mind, it should be pointed out that personal computers can be used in developmental activities that go beyond traditional education. For example, a relatively new career development software package will guide users through a number of steps that lead to a clarification of their career goals and qualifications, and then career plans will be generated by the software. The system not only teaches about career planning, it actually walks the user through the process. The PC acts as a tireless, always accessible consultant.

Other applications are also being developed. For example, decision-making software will ask questions necessary to help the user evaluate a problem, generate alternatives, and then make an optimal decision. Project management software will ask for data pertinent to a project at hand and then print out the charts or reports needed by the project manager. Text-editing software will scan a document, identify possible problem areas, and then suggest improvements. Clearly, the need for education in these areas has been reduced. The computer itself is taking the role of expert consultant.

Conclusion

Personal computers are helping to forge the future of education in business, and those changes will certainly be reflected in other continuing education settings. The subjects being taught are changing as computers change the way that people live and work. The efficiency of education continues to improve as computers extend the capabilities of administrators and educators, and educational effectiveness is increasing due to computerized presentation, interaction, illustration, and evaluation. The locus of educational responsibility is shifting from teacher to learner as more self-instruction and programmed learning options become available.

All this would seem to imply that the role of educator may be diminishing. It is not, although it is changing. Traditional teachers will be used less at NCR, and the things they teach will change to topics such as sales and supervision, where human interaction is a must. However, this small decline in the need for teachers will be more than offset by the tremendous need for course developers. Not only does rapidly changing technology increase the need for courseware but also the development of programmed courses is much more difficult than that of live courses. For example, one hour of interactive videodisk instruction requires over five times the development time necessary to produce one hour of live classroom instruction. These changes, forecast over twenty years ago in public education, are becoming a reality now, especially in corporations like NCR, IBM, Digital Equipment Corporation, and other companies that have the resources, expertise, and educational need to make these changes work.

John Thomasson earned his doctorate from the University of Arizona in higher education administration and is a senior curriculum development analyst at the NCR Management College in Dayton, Ohio.

Ronald Larsen is director of course development, evaluation, and instructional technology at the NCR Computer Science Institute in Dayton and is active in stimulating increased application of the personal computer as an educational tool.

*Following these suggestions can lead to successful
marketing of adult computer literacy programs.*

Adult Computer Literacy:
A Marketing Opportunity
with Financial Rewards

Sherrill L. Amador

The focus of this chapter is on marketing and financial implications of
continuing education as programs that teach adults to use the computer
as a tool. This marketing approach highlights target audiences, services
(curricular formats), promotional methods, and funding plans that have
been financially successful for adult continuing education programs at
Southwestern College and other educational institutions in San Diego
County, California.

The microcomputer revolution in the United States has created a
need for "adult computer literacy." By computer literacy I mean facility at
using the personal computer and more specifically at using software run
on the computer. However, one of the reasons that the personal-computer
hardware market may be experiencing leveling sales is that many users do
not know how to utilize the potential of the computer they own or presently operate.

Program success and increased tuition generation can be achieved
by providing adult computer literacy programs that respond to the market
audiences that want to realize the full potential of their computers. The
more diverse and responsive the programs are to the target markets, the

B. Heermann (Ed.). *Personal Computers and the Adult Learner.*
New Directions for Continuing Education, no. 29. San Francisco: Jossey-Bass, March 1986.

more successful they will be. Taking advantage of these market opportunities can be financially rewarding for adult continuing education programs.

Among factors fueling interest in learning about computers are the following:

- Employment requirements for nontechnical employees to have knowledge of computer technology (especially office workers, middle managers, and supervisors)
- A new generation of computer-literate children, which has developed through electronic games and formal computer education in elementary and secondary schools
- Heavy marketing by personal-computer companies
- Natural curiosity of adults to learn about the new technology and its impact on their lives
- The development of the personal computer as a status symbol.

The Adult Computer Literacy Market

The need for adult computer literacy has established a new continuing education market. The existence of a market for adult computer literacy programs can be traced to several realities of the personal computer marketplace. First, hardware and software manufacturers do not find it financially feasible to offer training programs on computer use or applications. Second, computer training within companies is not always a high priority. Needle (1985) states, "Unfortunately, many companies minimize the importance of training people in the rush to 'computerize' operations. As one computer instructor puts it: 'I've hardly ever seen an office where learning is a priority' " (pp. 101–102).

Third, retailers of personal computers offer limited training programs, usually no more than a few hours, which is not enough time for the user to become knowledgeable about computers. As Berger (1985) observes, "computer hardware manufacturers don't want to deal with training; neither do software makers. And retail dealers, if you get them aside and assure them they are speaking off the record, will tell you, 'We sell iron. We don't want to train people to use these things' " (p. I-1).

However, independent computer consultants advise users on how to buy and use hardware and software and there are plenty of them available, but they are an expensive training option for companies. And, finally, independent computer schools that focus on microcomputers have been a relative "bust."

Although the market for educating or training adults in how to use a computer exists, a satisfactory program is seldom adequately delivered to adult learners. Therefore, continuing educators have an opportunity to capitalize on the market for adult computer literacy education. These programs have a built-in potential for success because the learner market has already been created.

What are the characteristics, then, of the target market? The population of adult learners who are pursuing computer literacy is essentially the same group of adult learners profiled by Cross (1981): These learners are typically employed, have a higher than mean income, are women, and have previously participated in continuing education.

The adult learners who are attracted to computer literacy programs have generally been exposed through their work to the microcomputer, or they may have the foresight to acknowledge that computer skills will become a part of their jobs in the near future.

Nationally, business offices are being transformed by personal computers. Therefore, the working environment of the support staff is changing, which affect more women than men as women are in the majority in the office worker category.

Support staff personnel have been quick to see the benefits of learning to use the computer as a tool in the office for correspondence (word processing), financial applications (spread sheets), filing (data bases), and communication (graphics and telecommunications).

An above-average income is one characteristic of the continuing education participant. In the case of computer literacy, this is probably a more prominent factor because additional family income may be required to purchase personal computers, and above-average income people are more likely to be in jobs that require computer knowledge.

Southwestern College, a two-year public community college in Chula Vista, California, surveyed 245 adults who had completed its computer literacy education program and found the following characteristics, which are typical of adult learners in general:

- Average age: 32.11 years
- Percentage of students over twenty-one years of age: 92.3 percent
- Female: 67.92 percent
- Ethnic background (nonwhite): 49.03 percent (college nonwhite population in geographic region or district: 60 percent)
- Employed: 70.69 percent
- Percentage of students with family income over $20,000: 72.45 percent
- College districtwide family income: $15,657

Creating a Marketable Program

What type of program should be created to respond to this favorable market?

Instructional Methodology. To attract the adult learner to programs and courses that teach the use of the computer as a tool, certain scheduling and instructional methods have fared well based on student enrollments and continuing demand for courses. After reviewing several successful adult computer literacy programs, some trends are evident.

Small lectures or demonstrations with considerable lab time for hands-on experience with a computer are the most attractive to the adult learner. Programs without hands-on experience are not as successful.

A lab classroom formula of one adult to one computer is the ideal configuration, since it provides the learner with maximum time on each task. Other programs have found that two adults to one computer is instructionally sound and actually provides positive peer reinforcement. At Southwestern College, and in many other similar programs, the optimum class size is between twenty-five and thirty students.

Generally, there is a lecture and lab component for each course. The lecture component of the curriculum can be taught in the computer lab room in a demonstration mode, or it can be taught in a separate room as a stand-alone lecture to provide more access to computer labs for other classes and thus more efficient utilization of the computers. At Southwestern both methods have been used to determine which is the most effective instructionally. There does not seem to be any significant difference in learning or in adult perceptions of how much they learn whether the lecture is taught in the lab or in a separate lecture room.

The majority of schools in this region that offer adult computer literacy programs indicated that a more formal closed lab setting is more conducive to adult learning than an open lab where students come in whenever it is convenient for them to work on the computer. However, there should be time available, if at all possible, for an open lab for the adult learner to accommodate additional practice and allow extra time for different learning rates. This is especially critical if students do not have access to a computer at work or in their homes.

Course Sequence and Content. The course sequence may begin with an overview of the operation and uses of a microcomputer. Major emphasis should be on the applications potential of the computer with the student being provided some experience with word processing, spread sheets, and data-base software packages. A simple program may be presented to teach the differences between software and programming. General terminology is also presented in the initial course.

Typically, the courses that follow are on specific software applications. The instructor uses hands-on application problems or lab assignments and activities to introduce content as well as to evaluate learning. The additional software applications include at least one course on word processing and a second course on advanced text editing using word processing software.

Word processing is the most widely used application of microcomputers; therefore, it is the most logical second course in any program.

A common sequence then includes one course on spread sheets, with additional courses integrating data-base, word processing, and graphics packages. A separate course on data bases and possibly an advanced data-base course are recommended.

Courses on programming languages are still in demand, with BASIC being the most generally offered language, although the trend is to put less emphasis on programming, with many curricula presenting no programming language courses at all as the need for instruction in popular software programs escalate.

Markets Requiring Special Courses. To meet the diverse audiences attracted to adult computer literacy, continuing educators may design special programs. The following paragraphs describe several examples.

Computer Literacy for Elementary and Secondary Teachers. Programs should incorporate courses in LOGO, software evaluation, and teaching methodology using computers. This course should be taught by an elementary or secondary school teacher.

Contract Education for Special Employee Groups. In this case, the employer pays for the program. Program directors need to respond quickly to create a specific computer curriculum to meet the training specifications of the company. Having a competency-based curriculum for the adult computer literacy program provides the needed flexibility to respond to these employee requests for special course configurations (fewer class hours, unique applications, and specific employee classifications).

Small-Business Microcomputer Applications Courses. These should include the areas of accounting and budgeting, scheduling, inventory control, and personnel record keeping. The small-business entrepreneur is one of the largest purchasers of microcomputer hardware and software, and manufacturers advertise heavily for this market, yet this group generally has little knowledge of the effective and efficient uses of the microcomputer.

Scheduling Formats. The total hours of instruction for the courses range from fifteen to thirty. Adult students usually request more class time, even though initially the shorter time period is more attractive to them. The duration of the class, in terms of number of weeks, is also something the market responds to. Friday or Saturday classes are very successful.

Southwestern College's most popular format is three weekends in a row with a course that is offered three hours on Friday evening and six hours on Saturday, for a total of twenty-seven hours. A five-course computer literacy or microcomputer applications certificate can be earned within a single semester. Courses that are in four-week and six-week configurations are also well received when they are offered in an evening format, meeting twice per week.

Certificates of Completion. Higher education institutions in the San Diego area have found that offering a certificate for special groupings of courses or individual courses is a marketing strategy that encourages adult participation. Increasingly, employers are asking for such a certificate. Also, adults want certificates as proof of their newly acquired skills, and these certificates should be attractive and professional looking, with an appropriate logo, signatures, and course information. Having course competencies listed on the back of the certificates is appreciated by employers and gives the graduated students a worthwhile document for seeking promotions or new positions.

College credit for these courses is not a requirement; however, the availability of that option is well received by students who have prior degrees or who work for employers who give pay increases based on continuing education or college credit units.

Advertising to the Appropriate Market. Several methods have been successful for advertising adult computer literacy programs.

- Direct mailings of program brochures to lists of previous continuing education students
- Direct mailings of the college class schedules to the community, which include special sections for adult continuing education programs
- Personal contacts by continuing education program representatives with company and government agency officials to promote programs in two ways: as a potential employee-training program paid for by the company, and to gain permission to circulate brochures directly to employees
- Direct mailing of brochures to local companies, industries, government agenies, service clubs, and computer hardware and software retailers and distributors
- Presentations by continuing education program representatives at various group meetings (for example, service clubs and professional organizations)
- Advertisements in company newsletters, local newspapers, professional and union associations newsletters, and local periodicals
- Promotion through local chambers of commerce and the Small-Business Administration Agency in an effort to reach the entrepreneur.

The brochures and ads need to be focused on the potential adult learner or the employer. These brochures and ads should be very professional, as these audiences will be more attracted to that kind of advertising. The awarding of certificates for the program or courses should be stressed. Giving the names of computers and software used (if they are the most heavily marketed brands by manufacturers) can be an effective promotional technique. The use of previously suggested scheduling formats and instructional methods are attractive features that should be stressed in the promotional materials.

Financing a Good Marketing Idea

Southwestern's computer literacy program is part of a larger marketing strategy to encourage enrollment, thereby increasing revenue at the college. These new computer literacy courses have resulted in a considerable increase in the number of students over the previous year. However, responding to the attractive opportunity that the adult computer literacy market provides can be a difficult problem for continuing education program directors when expensive equipment and software are required.

Revenue Sources. For those programs that are operated by extension units of universities and colleges, the user typically must bear the cost. Typical costs for a computer literacy course in the San Diego area range from $295 for fifteen hours of extension instruction to $5 for twenty-seven hours of instruction in a community college class. The difference in cost to the adult student is due to the fact that the community college may offer the course for credit and receive state aid based on weekly student contact hours, whereas the noncredit extension programs are free financed.

It should be noted that the difference in course cost is not a significant factor in attracting adult students. There are five educational institutions offering similar programs within this wide range of costs to students in San Diego: The University of California-San Diego (UCSD) and San Diego State University (SDSU) offer extension programs; National University, a private college, offers an extension program; and Grossmont and Southwestern colleges, both two-year community colleges, offer college credit programs. Yet each of these five programs is successful in terms of student enrollments.

Finance Plans. An exceptionally high student demand for adult computer literacy programs caused by a strong market creates a favorable situation for program financing. Tuition revenue can be generated quickly to offset the initial capital outlay for purchasing computer equipment and software.

For example, at Southwestern College, a computer lab was created specifically to operate the computer literacy program. It is located in an existing building that required minor modifications and a total capital outlay of $131,000 to purchase thirty microcomputers and thirty copies of word processing, data-base, spread-sheet programs. The $131,000 was a relatively modest outlay as a result of vendor and manufacturing discounts for educational institutions.

Selection of Hardware and Software. The costs of hardware and software can be kept to a minimum by using one brand of microcomputer and one brand of each of the software packages. The selection of the software for Southwestern College was determined by what were the best sellers nationally in the previous year, even though other brands may have been given higher ratings for specific features. Program developers felt that students would be more attracted to the brands that were used at their workplace or that they personally had purchased because of effective advertising by the manufacturer. By using known brand names (Lotus 1-2-3, Wordstar, Visacalc, DBase III, Apple MacIntosh, and IBM PC) in course descriptions and in program promoting, the college benefits from the association with these known brands. The hardware and software companies advertise heavily in personal computing and business periodicals and newspapers. When potential students see these ads, they associate the name with the adult computer literacy program advertised by the college or university.

As effective network and hard disk systems become available, cost savings can be realized in software purchases and site license agreements. Southwestern College, after one year of operation of the computer literacy program, had recovered all hardware, software, and direct teaching salary costs and still realized an additional $20,000 in tuition revenue. All future tuition revenue earned will be debited only by direct instructional and maintenance costs. The college has an on-campus computer maintenance degree program whose students service all equipment as part of their cooperative work-experience class. Some colleges have work-study students trained for routine maintenance as well.

Additional Funding Sources. When extension programs do not have capital outlay funds to purchase computers, then arrangements can be made with the associated college or university to use their labs. This places some programs at a disadvantage because, if the college or university has priorities for instructional computing within the credit curriculum, that program usually receives priority lab usage. Local continuing education program directors indicated that, through reserve funds, they had accumulated sufficient resources to create their own labs and plan through student demand to recoup the initial costs of offering their programs. Lease agreements can be made with local vendors for hardware; these agreements can include reduced rates for vendor customers who attend the adult computer literacy program.

A Start-Up Program. A well-marketed adult computer literacy program with an initial equipment configuration of ten microcomputers with two students to a computer and ten copies of appropriate software can form the basis for new revenue for most existing continuing education programs. The key to success is for the program director to analyze the potential market, determine what competition is already present, and then make the new program distinctive and responsive to the market audience.

References

Berger, D. "Unique Approach a Success." *San Diego Union.* May 19, 1985, p. I-1.
Cross, K. P. *Adults as Learners: Increasing Participation and Facilitating Learning.* San Francisco: Jossey-Bass, 1981.
Needle, D. "The Smart Way to Learn Computing." *Personal Computing.* 1985, *9* (6), 101–106.

Sherrill L. Amador is the dean of the business instructional division at Southwestern College. She was the administrator responsible for creating the college's successful computer literacy program.

Data communications and computer conferencing
are two major uses of computers waiting to be
explored and incorporated throughout the continuing
education field.

The Computer as a Networking and Information Resource for Adult Learners

Ben R. H. Davis
Catherine L. Marlowe

When adult learners using computers are linked together through devices called modems and telephone lines, a network is created enabling micro-computers to communicate with one another or with much larger main-frame computers. Presently, most comunications between computers focus on data communications—transferring facts, figures, and text. Simultaneous voice and data transmission is now available; individuals may speak with one another about computer files of text and data each is receiving and viewing at the time of the conversation. This technological advance alone justifies the exploration of computer applications to continuing education. But much is readily available to enhance teaching and learning in the field.

The development of data communications has led to a variety of information-retrieval services and computer conferencing systems. Of course, many are directly applicable to professionals in the field, but they also serve learners, who, because of other important responsibilities involving their work and families, need to maximize flexibility in their available time for

B. Heermann (Ed.). *Personal Computers and the Adult Learner.*
New Directions for Continuing Education, no. 29. San Francisco: Jossey-Bass, March 1986.

learning. Subject matter content and learning methods are likely to be profoundly affected by the increasing use of computers as a learning resource.

With over 1,800 data bases or information-retrieval services available to continuing education students and instructors, the resource options are almost endless. Some serve highly specialized audiences, but others are very useful sources of learning. Three major information services, Dialog, CompuServe, and The Source, and one computer conferencing system, Electronic Information Exchange System, (EIES), illustrate the extensive diversity of data communications and their usefulness for continuing education professionals and students. One application of computer conferencing, TeleLearning, specifically addresses credit and noncredit courses for higher and continuing education.

Information Services and Computer Conferencing

The Dialog Information Retrieval Service, begun in 1972, operates more than 130 data bases in its system with more than fifty million records on file and accessible to the computer user covering a wide variety of subjects. One of Dialog's data bases, the Educational Resources Information Center (ERIC), consists of over half a million citations of educational resource materials. MARC and REMARC are data bases containing over six million records representing the catalogued collections of the United States Library of Congress. For continuing education, this represents on-line access to a comprehensive, worldwide collection of materials, which can be searched from home, office, or university by author, title, subject, series, publication date, or even a single word or phrase. Other Dialog data bases cover many fields of science, medicine, and engineering, and one contains information on foundation gifts and grants.

CompuServe Information Services focuses on contemporary information and offers an Associated Press on-line news service. Through this service the Official Airline Guide can be read and air and ground reservations made for business or pleasure without travel agents. CompuServe's communication features provide any individual the opportunity to receive and send electronic messages and mail, as well as joining in computer conferencing with other subscribers. This service also includes home shopping, banking services, and games.

The Source, described as "America's information utility," is similar to CompuServe with its news service from the United Press International wire, message sending and receiving capabilities, as well as daily business and financial news. It also offers shopping services and games. The Source helps individuals find others who share professional interests, and it networks computer users to serve their hardware and software needs.

Electronic systems, like CompuServe and The Source, provide access to extensive information for individuals and organizations. The service is organized to encourage computer users to explore the various information options. Time and distance are no constraints for any learner who incorporates access to these information systems in his or her courses of study.

While there are a number of computer conferencing systems, the earliest and most widely known system is the Electronic Information Exchange System (EIES). This system was initiated in 1971 when wage and price controls were imposed by President Nixon, and it was necessary to maintain contact with a large number of people dispersed throughout the country needing answers to many issues at all times of day and night. As questions arose regarding administration policies and practices, communication to all requiring the information was not possible through use of the telephone or the postal service. The EIES computer conferencing system helped establish consistent policies and provided timely information on wage and price controls.

Today, EIES is a more advanced system, and its design can assure that continuing education professionals and learners work together and communicate on a regular basis. It provides electronic mail services and ongoing computer conferences similar to other information services. However, it also includes private work space for developing one's thoughts before transmitting to other conference members. EIES gives word, text, and document processing capability to individuals and groups for the creation and distribution of reports and papers. It can customize communication services so that specialized groups of individuals in continuing education can concentrate on a particular problem. Access to additional data bases is available through EIES and enables subscribers to participate in voting and surveys. EIES is especially appropriate for the continuing education professional or learner who desires to participate in state-of-the-art conferencing with geographically dispersed colleagues. Among users of EIES and other computer conferencing systems, a strong camaraderie develops, although TeleLearning, a corporation developing a computer conferencing educational system, is specifically geared to adult learners who are computer users. TeleLearning, or the "electronic university," is creating a telecommunication network designed for education, and all family members can participate in a wide variety of courses both for college credit and not for credit. With over 100 courses presently offered, students pursue study in many subject areas. Instructors are "on line" to assist learners in mastering course materials. Those involved in TeleLearning courses, and most of these are adults, illustrate the applicability of telecommunications to serve the growing need in continuing education for easy access to new skills and knowledge.

Continuing Education Applications

Professionals and learners face a variety of options when seeking to incorporate data communications and electronic networking in educational programs. One obvious use of telecommunications is for information retrieval. Given the great number and accessibility of data bases, an individual does not need to spend significant amounts of time researching materials in public and university libraries. With the ability to search through millions of documents looking for specific words or phrases, or seeking information on very specific topics, many more sources will be discovered than by an individual searching in libraries. One reality of computerized information retrieval, however, is that it is expensive. On-line costs vary widely, but staff and students should allocate about $100 an hour for information retrieved through most computer searches.

One method of avoiding the high costs of data searches is to make extensive use of public bulletin boards created by individuals and organizations throughout the country. Every metropolitan area has a number of bulletin boards that can be accessed by the computer's modem. These no- or low-cost electronic boards permit the sending and receiving of mail and messages for any number of participants. All offer access to important information sources of interest to computer users. Public electronic bulletin boards provide individuals with specialized and general information on an amazing number of topics.

Continuing education professionals and learners can now make extensive use of telecommunications for sending and receiving electronic mail. Regardless of a learner's location, contact can be initiated and maintained with individuals or organizations with similar interests throughout the country or the world. With careful planning to utilize public bulletin boards, individuals are able to enjoy the benefits of the technology while avoiding the high costs.

Computer-assisted instruction and computer-based training are also clearly applicable to continuing education students and staff engaged in electronic networking activities. Computer-assisted instruction combined with the availability of electronic networking means additional applications for computer courses that have been developed for independent learner use. Computer-based training, which incorporates an instructor as well as computer programs and often workbooks, is another way to involve adult learners with computers and the world of electronic networking. In these situations, the technology is a new, complementary teaching tool. Whatever the format, computer instruction is accomplished through a hands-on approach so that individuals learn by doing, not simply listening and watching.

What are the unique advantages of communicating via computers rather than simply writing a letter or making a telephone call? A letter takes days to reach its destination, sometimes weeks, and once in a while it never arrives at all. Also a letter or report arrives pretty much in an unchangeable form. Few people rewrite a letter, and reports can be rewritten only with considerable effort. Reports and letters received electronically over the telephone wires between computers can be easily modified and shared.

A telephone call, a form of technology we now take for granted, is an important and effective means of communications. Our voices transmitted over telephone lines convey emotional states and significant, even though limited, amounts of hard data. Telephone calls facilitate decision making; consequently, records of phone calls are included in any well-managed office. Lengthy reports are seldom read over the phone; tables with columns and rows of figures are less often communicated via telephone. And graphic images such as the layout of a room are not easily transmitted over the telephone. One soon realizes the truth that "a picture is worth more than a thousand words."

Thus, telephone conversations alone are inadequate for complex discussions involving large numbers of facts and figures or long reports. Individuals usually wait until the written material is at hand before participating in telephone conversations regarding it. Finally, the party called must be available for a telephone conversation to take place. The frustrating and time-consuming "telephone tag" process is eliminated with electronic mail.

Continuing education professionals and students are "naturals" for active participation in interactive telecomputing and electronic conferencing. Because adults usually have rich and varied experiences, they have much to share with others via their computers. The world of computer conferencing is just opening to adult learners, and through it, extensive networking activities can be undertaken and augmented as mutual interests are discovered and acted upon.

In the world of telecomputing, data communications are learning-centered activities. Each person learns from direct experience with data bases and conferencing systems. Even when widely and inexpensively available, simultaneous voice and data transmission will only constitute a small proportion of total telecommunication activities. The ability to receive and transmit a wide variety of text, data, and graphics makes owning and using a computer more worthwhile. Continuing education incorporation of data communications leads to even greater use of this new technology and extends programs far beyond classroom settings.

Conclusion

With electronic networking, continuing education professionals and learners no longer have to sift through mountains of paperwork and literature to find needed data. Information retrieved by the computer can be stored by the computer, ready for further use at any time. Slowly, computer access is replacing the card catalogue at the University of California, Berkeley, library, and students search the collection electronically. Entering a few keystrokes provides immediate access to current topics and available resource materials rather than browsing library stacks, flipping pages in reference books, or struggling with microfiche.

94

Telephone calls and mail service remain important communication links for individuals and organizations. Computers will not replace these means of communication. However, telephone calls and letters are supplemented by electronic mail simply because it is faster, more efficient, and every interaction is recorded for further reference.

While many adults work independently at their own pace in a number of locations, significant learning also takes place in group settings. Continuing education programs carry out much of their important work through group participation. And, of course, many adult learners choose familiar classroom settings, duplicating earlier learning modes experienced in elementary and secondary school. For learners in remote locations, however, finding sufficient members to form an interest or learning group may not be possible. The introduction of computers and telecommunications enables individuals to work in groups, thus sustaining an important and familiar learning dimension.

Continuing education professionals who design programs for adult learners utilizing computers are sensitive to incorporating group dynamics into the planning and execution of educational programs. Individualized and self-paced telecommunication-based programs can incorporate group activities quite easily, enabling learning to embrace the best of both worlds. Computers, through teleconferencing and electronic mail, can readily serve groups of interested learners as well as they serve individuals in an office or at home.

In the last analysis, individuals operate computers. Individuals also telecommunicate with them. Continuing educators' attitudes toward these electronic machines are considerably varied, fluctuating between love and hate for how they look, what they can do, and how fast they perform. The computer is an important ally for professionals and learners since it increases productivity, encourages experimentation, and supports trial and error in utilizing the tool for telecommunications. The computer reduces isolation, enabling colleagues and learners to make contact and keep in touch with one another. Networking with computers promotes the development of special-interest groups and expands one's circle of professional contacts and friends. Active participation by continuing education students and staff in telecommunications means being at the edge of contemporary technology, learning from those experiences, and incorporating new principles and products appropriately into the field.

Ben R. H. Davis is a professor with the Union for Experimenting Colleges and Universities.

Catherine L. Marlowe is a technical writer for GTE Sprint Communications.

New concepts of "teaching" and "learning" are required for optimal use of microcomputers in continuing education programs.

Microcomputers and Adult Learning: Maximizing Potentials

Barry G. Sheckley

The uses of microcomputers described in this volume illustrate wide-ranging potentials for enhancing continuing education programs. In an insightful opening chapter, Barry Heermann describes three continuing education strategies for employing personal computers as: *teaching machines* to help learn new material (examples include drill-and-practice, tutorials, and self-assessment programs); *learning tools* to promote formation of new ideas (such as word processors, data-base programs, and spread sheets); and *learning resources* to access information (for example, computer networks, on-line data-base services, and computer bulletin boards). This chapter elaborates on that organizing framework, then analyzes optimal computer uses in our technologically advanced and information-rich society. The central thesis here, as throughout this volume, is that microcomputers as learning resources and learning tools represent a particularly appropriate technology to enhance continuing education. Operational principles for effective use of microcomputers in continuing education programs based on current adult learning research, including illustrative examples from each chapter, will also be presented.

B. Heermann (Ed.). *Personal Computers and the Adult Learner.*
New Directions for Continuing Education, no. 29. San Francisco: Jossey-Bass, March 1986.

Microcomputers as Teaching Machines

Microcomputers are commonly employed as teaching machines for drill and practice, teaching terms or languages, presenting problems, and diagnosing weaknesses (Kulik, Kulik, and Cohen, 1980). The infernally patient machines present information, pose questions and problems, accept answers, evaluate responses, and provide remedial instruction.

Personal computers are widely used for computer-assisted instruction since they are such effective teaching machines. Decreases of 30 percent or more in information acquisition times are consistently attributed to computer-assisted instruction (Fauley, 1983). For example, Kemper Insurance, in conducting a cost-benefit analysis of computer-assisted instruction, showed an overall 65 percent reduction in training time. A simulation-based microcomputer program for training Falcon Jet cockpit procedures cut training time by more than two-thirds, reduced training cost per participant by more than $20,000, and was rated highly effective by trainees and supervisors.

John Thomasson and Ronald Larsen (Chapter Eight) provide especially illuminating illustrations of computers as teaching machines. At National Cash Register (NCR), computer-assisted instruction enables students to complete courses in programming in five hours when more traditional self-paced methods require twelve hours. Also at NCR, self-paced computer-programmed learning allows field engineers to complete their studies from 30 to 50 percent faster than through traditional classroom instruction to levels of interactive and individualized training not possible with traditional classroom methods.

Effectiveness of computer-assisted instruction results from several factors, including levels of interactivity no teacher can match (D'Angelo, 1979). Individualized instruction (that is, matching the learning interests of students with serially presented instruction) is a primary computer-assisted instruction attribute. Computers used as teaching machines allow individuals to move at their own pace, are generally available when learners want to use them, enable learners to adapt learning materials to personal interests, readily "tolerate" mistakes, and provide immediate feedback. The flexibility of computer-assisted instruction also contributes to wide-ranging applications, from using LOGO, to teach adults skills in learning how to learn, to enhancing management skills with Thoughtware modules (Chapters Three and Six).

Computers also provide effective ways to augment limited instructional resources. Reporting on a computerized tutorial used in the Open University, Gerver (1984) notes that students appreciate many aspects of the computerized operation, including individualized teaching, more course material, a tutor who could not get sidetracked, immediate feedback, and provisions for self-assessment. At Cernitin America (see Chapter

Six), ingenious use of computer-assisted instruction options allowed a small company to provide management training without hiring additional training staff.

Despite strong potentials for skill training and selective information acquisition, microcomputer use cannot be limited to teaching machines in an information-rich and technologically advanced society. Strange (1983) warns that continued emphases on computer-assisted instruction designs will restrict innovative uses of computers. Further, such stultification will hinder the impact microcomputers could have in altering traditional definitions of learning and teaching. To achieve full benefits from using computer technology, continuing education programs need to develop microcomputer potentials as learning tools and learning resources.

Microcomputers as Learning Tools

Microcomputer spread sheets, word processors, and data bases are powerful learning tools that help learners to perform complex computations, formulate ideas, and analyze information. Currently, such uses are not common among continuing education programs. A recent issue of *Technological Horizons in Education* (March 1985), which explored computer uses in this sphere of education, included only one example of microcomputers as this type of learning tool. Uses of computer-assisted instruction dominated the journal, as they do the field of continuing education.

This sourcebook provides several illustrations of computers used as processors of information to facilitate the formation of creative ideas. At NCR, for example, word processing is described as indispensable to course developers. Individualization of student evaluations is enhanced by NCR instructors using word processing to adapt standardized forms so they reflect the strengths and weaknesses of particular students. Computer networking capabilities provide communication tools enabling NCR curriculum specialists and graphic artists to work in project teams developing instructional materials.

Sandra Ratcliff (Chapter Five) provides a fascinating overview of the creative use of computers at the Center for Law and Computers. Access to this technology has enhanced the abilities of law students in learning law and in developing those analytical skills now so necessary for forensic undertakings. In continuing legal education, computers are used as tools for information management, assembling or revising legal documents, and organizing information with legal spread sheets.

Microcomputers as learning tools support the development of such learning skills as problem solving, decision making, information analysis, and creativity. They make information readily available and increase the efficiency of adult learners in learning, controlling, and organizing information. Gerver (1984) suggests that this may be the greatest role microcomputers play since it alleviates such tedious activities as memorization or hunting for information. With microcomputers as learning tools, adults spend more time on creative integrative learning and idea formation and less time on calculating statistical formulas, computing spread-sheet totals, and retyping manuscripts.

Adults eagerly use computers as learning tools since they enable individualized approaches to idea formation. For example, lawyers at the Center for Law and Computers readily used word processors and electronic spread sheets during computer lab time to supplement continuing education courses. Availability of computer learning tools might even increase participation in continuing education programs by promoting self-directed opportunities for idea formation. Research consistently documents the preferences adult learners have for planning their own learning projects, with defining content, controlling pace, and establishing style being particularly important (Tough, 1979).

Computerized learning tools enable adults to study an extraordinarily wide range of situations. Simulations help learners form ideas about phenomena otherwise difficult to explore. For example, using popular flight simulator programs, an adult can experiment with flight maneuvers in a risk-free manner. At NCR, personal computer simulations are used for software developers to manipulate productivity tools necessary in programming mainframe computers; these protect valuable computer files until error-free procedures are developed and implemented.

Microcomputers as Learning Resources

Microcomputers as learning resources have great potential for continuing education. Ivan Illich (1970) discusses ideal educational systems as "opportunity webs" that provide: (1) access to things (such as books or maps) or processes (such as statistical programs) used in learning; (2) skill exchanges that match teachers and learners; (3) peer matching networks that permit individuals to find partners for inquiry; and (4) reference services that provide master guides for difficult exploratory inquiries.

Networking arrangements provide access to information data banks and the collective wisdom of other learners. As summarized in Chapter Ten, data bases and information services available through national computer networks (such as The Source or CompuServe) illustrate the multiple information resource options such computer networks provide. Computer networks also provide access to other learners as information resources. Recently a group of continuing educators from various regions of the country used the Electronic Information Exchange System (EIES) to develop improved learner services for adults. The computer network represented a unique information exchange since the data base of knowledge resided in the experience of each participant.

Uses of computers to establish information exchanges may have great potential for continuing education. Consider this scenario based on my personal experiences with computer networks. A continuing education director, plagued with low enrollments in independent study courses, discovers that adult students are having difficulty meeting with their assigned professors. With electronic mail and bulletin board arrangements available through the campus computer center, the director creates mainframe computer files for teaching. Students and professors can access these files either with campus-based terminals or with modems and home computers. An exciting information network soon emerges. Early semester question-and-answer exchanges rapidly change as students begin answering questions that other students address to the professor and seminal dialogues evolve. By midsemester, the teacher-student relationship blurs as students and professors seek information from each other as reciprocal information resources. The innovative computer network quickly develops as a highly successful continuing education offering.

Uses of computers to establish such information exchanges may have great potential for continuing education. With these innovative designs, computer courses may be the most effective way yet discovered for making continuing education responsive to adults with diverse background and heterogeneous interests.

The greatest potential for microcomputers may be to provide liberating access to information. The computer, as an information storage and retrieval tool, provides adult learners with convenient and rapid access to information that has the potential to assist them to reflect on, understand, and perhaps change their world. Continuing education seeks to empower adults by enabling them to manipulate information through reading, writing, computing, and related skills. As Heaney (1982) argues, microcomputers could become a force to negotiate shifts in social power by decentralizing information control and providing open information access to the public. From this perspective, information access may provide disenfranchised adults with a vehicle to blur status relationships and increase individual or collective power. Some analysts (such as Strange, 1983) say this represents the greatest possibility for computers as learning resources.

Maximizing Potentials

How can microcomputers be best used in continuing education programs? Should programs emphasize computers as learning machines, learning tools, or learning resources? While computer-assisted instruction is well suited for information acquisition, microcomputers as learning tools and learning resources are particularly appropriate for what Kolb (1984) terms the higher-order integrative learning tasks characteristic of adult learning.

Microcomputers as learning tools and learning resources provide enhanced potentials for continuing education in an information-rich and technologically advanced age. To realize these potentials, continuing education programs need to employ three guiding principles. First, innovative concepts of teaching and learning need to be adopted to maximize microcomputer potentials. Second, adult learners should be trusted to use microcomputer options to their fullest advantage. Third, microcomputers should be combined with group activities in high-tech/high-touch configurations. The following subsections elaborate on each of these principles.

Innovative Concepts of Teaching and Learning. New concepts of teaching and learning are required to realize optimal uses of microcomputers as learning tools and learning resources. In Chapter Ten, Davis and Marlowe creatively set a context for continuing education in an age characterized by readily accessible information. Dede (1981) suggests that technological innovations will change current definitions of intelligence to provide a greater emphasis on analysis, synthesis, and evaluation. As information becomes easily accessible through technology, the skills of selecting the best options from many choices, analyzing implications, synthesizing information with other knowledge, and evaluating outcomes will be crucial to successful intellectual endeavors. Microcomputers as sources of information for adults could release education from its historically primary role of transmitting information from source to learner, and they are likely to transform definitions of teaching and learning. Apps (1982) suggests that microcomputers could make teaching and learning more than transmission and acquisition of information. If continuing education could be liberated from primary reliance on the passive transmission of information, participants could spend more time on the meaning of new input, on problems and issues, on ethical concerns, and on matters that require creative deliberation.

Traditional instruction models have had teachers assume major responsibility for developing, structuring, and evaluating student learning projects. This traditional role is based on the presumed responsibilities of teachers to teach and of students to learn what teachers teach. A more sophisticated teaching model may be appropriate for effective use of microcomputers in continuing education programs.

Research on adult learning implies that roles for teachers of adults should shift from providers and evaluators of all learning to facilitators who teach learning processes, develop critical judgment, guide self-managed options, and provide evaluative standards for adult learning projects (Sheckley, 1985). Kolb (1984) discusses learning as a process of creating knowledge by acquiring information through experience and abstraction, then transforming it through reflection and active experimentation. He describes how many continuing education approaches emphasize acquisition of knowledge and do not provide for the transformation of raw information into heuristic frameworks that enhance personal choice. If continuing educators adopt instructional models appropriate for adult learners in an information age, microcomputers could be used as learning tools and learning resources assisting adults to acquire and transform information in the process of creating new knowledge. One ironic implication of the foregoing discussion is that instructors must assume the role of adult learners while mastering the requisite computer technology.

Examples in this sourcebook demonstrate that effective microcomputer use begins with focused faculty development that stresses new and different concepts of teaching and learning. Hollowood (Chapter Two), in his discussion of designing microcomputer facilities, highlights the importance of faculty development in establishing computer-based curricula that enhance student-directed learning. Similarly, a foundation for the Health Education Network (Chapter Four) was instituted through a focus on faculty development that included emphasis on adult learning processes. Related research (for example, Hortin, 1982) indicates that the greatest obstacle to educational use of microcomputers is lack of teacher knowledge about differing applications. In reviewing reasons why microcomputers were not used in adult learning processes, Hausmann (1979) listed "lack of faculty training" (32 percent) as predominant over "lack of equipment" (22 percent), "lack of funds" (12 percent), "lack of time" (12 percent), "lack of interest" (11 percent), and "no application" (10 percent). To achieve the potential microcomputers have, faculty development needs to go beyond types and uses of software to grapple with the new ideas of teaching and learning that microcomputers can foster.

Trusting the Integrity of Adult Learners. A second principle for using microcomputers involves trusting adult learners to use learning resources to the best and fullest advantage. Meierhenry (1982) argues that current practice forces adult learners to adopt styles and strategies appropriate to traditionally passive undergraduates and that it does not allow for adapting microcomputers to the styles preferred by adult learners. Adults, as pragmatic learners, require a match between their learning objectives and those set by the instructional program. Standardized learning programs are not always appropriate for adult learners. Continuing education programs using microcomputers need to allow for self-planned options.

Throughout this sourcebook, the authors describe how adults, presented with reasonable alternatives, are remarkably adaptive in using microcomputers appropriately. Repeatedly, Hollowood (Chapter Two) cautions against imposing administrative solutions. In designing a microcomputer facility, he voiced the common concern about developing optimal lab schedules, purchasing an appropriate mix of computer hardware, and assuring that software packages were readily available. He concluded that such concerns were largely unfounded. Continuing education students effectively distributed themselves among various options without assistance of administrative policies.

The lesson carries over to instructional programs, as illustrated by several authors in this volume. When faculty at Ferris State College creatively employed a high-tech/high-touch approach to using microcomputers (Chapter Three) students designed an effective instructional module on group decision making. Warfield provides a stimulating discussion of how students used a movie production approach in developing a captivating Antarctica survival simulation. Similarly Wagner and Heermann, in a thought-provoking case study (Chapter Six), depict the self-motivating character of adult learners. They describe how employees at Cernitin America went beyond initial computer-assisted instruction options to design efficient self-development programs. While these applications illustrate important variations in using computer technology, they reveal only the tip of the iceberg when placed in the larger context of adult learning.

Research on adult learning projects consistently highlights the abilities of adult learners to plan their own learning. In a decade of research beginning in the 1970s, Tough (1979) investigated patterns of adult learning. He validated that the average adult spent 700 to 800 hours each year (or fifteen hours each week) completing eight learning projects. Adults he studied were more likely to use self-planned (73 percent) as opposed to either group-planned (14 percent) or one-to-one helper-planned (13 percent) approaches in completing learning projects. Research projects initiated by Allen Tough (1979) and replicated in many studies (such as Sheckley, 1985) challenge continuing educators to change their limiting perspectives on adult learning.

The examples in this volume, coupled with research on adult learning, have important implications for utilizing microcomputers in continuing education programs. Since adults have demonstrated tendencies to manage their own learning projects, continuing education programs should provide multiple options for using microcomputers. Adults can be trusted to determine their own optimal approaches and need not conform to established courses of instruction so as to meet the learning goals others demand of them.

Using High-Tech/High-Touch Approaches. Throughout the examples cited in this sourcebook, microcomputers as teaching machines, learning tools, and learning resources are used in combination with other learning strategies such as group exercises or group discussions. Computers employed as isolated teaching machines—and not as part of a group-oriented learning strategy—are criticized because they cannot provide the warmth and social interaction possible when groups of people work together. Many have difficulty thinking of computer-assisted instruction as developing attitudes and feelings about what it means to be human, developing ethical decision making, or developing appreciation for arts and humanities.

Naisbitt (1982) describes high-tech/high-touch combinations as a "megatrend" in current society. According to his analysis, each successful introduction of high technology (such as life-extending technology in hospitals) is balanced by a humanistic counterpart (such as the hospice movement). Using microcomputers in high-tech/high-touch combinations addressess many of the criticisms levied against them and markedly enhances their use in continuing education programs.

The high-tech/high-touch principle is the foundation for several of the exemplary programs described in this volume. Warfield, in Chapter Three, provides a sophisticated description of how Ferris State College combines high-tech computer-assisted instruction with high-touch team assignments and interactive supervisory exercises to train managers. The Antarctica survival exercise that her students developed offers a particularly illuminating illustration of a high-tech/high-touch combination. The creative applications described by Ratcliff in Chapter Five demonstrate how student camaraderie and cooperation were important ingredients in the successful Center for Law and Computers. Even Davis and Marlowe acknowledge, in arguments supporting computer networks (Chapter Ten), that adult learners are social beings who do not enjoy activities requiring extended isolation. Computer networks, according to this insightful analysis, are attractive means for adults in remote locations to interact with other learners.

Summary

Microcomputers have wide-ranging potentials for enhancing continuing education programs. While use of microcomputers as teaching machines (as in computer-aided instruction programs) receive the most attention, microcomputers as learning tools (as in word processing) or learning resources (as in computer networks) have tremendous potential for enhancing continuing education programs. This chapter has synthesized the examples provided in this sourcebook into three principles to guide continuing educators in realizing the educational potentials of microcomputers.

References

Apps, J. "Forward." In D. Gueulette (Ed.), *Microcomputers for Adult Learning: Potentials and Perils.* Chicago: Follett, 1982.

D'Angelo, J. "The Microprocessor as Pencil." *Association for Educational Data Systems Monitor,* 1979, *18,* 14–17.

Dede, C. "Educational, Social, and Ethical Implications of Technological Innovation." *Programmed Learning and Educational Technology,* 1981, *18* (4), 204-213.

Fauley, F. "The New Training Technologies: Their Rocky Road to Acceptance." *Training and Development Journal,* December 1983, pp. 22-25.

Gerver, E. *Computers and Adult Learning.* Stoney Stratford, Milton Keynes, U.K.: Open University Press, 1984.

Hausmann, K. "Instructional Computing in Higher Education." *AEDS Monitor,* 1979, *18* (5), 32-37.

Heaney, T. "Power, Learning, and Communication." In D. Gueulette (Ed.), *Microcomputers for Adult Learning: Potentials and Perils.* Chicago: Follett, 1982.

Hortin, J. "Information Resources for Computer-Assisted Instruction." In D. Gueulette (Ed.), *Microcomputers for Adult Learning: Potentials and Perils.* Chicago: Follett, 1982.

Illich, I. *Deschooling Society.* New York: Harper & Row, 1970.

Kolb, D. *Experiential Learning.* Englewood Cliffs, N.J.: Prentice-Hall, 1984.

Kulik, J. A., Kulik, C., and Cohen, P. "Effectiveness of Computer-Based College Teaching: A Meta-Analysis of Findings." *Review of Educational Research,* 1980, *50* (4), 525-544.

Meierhenry, W. C. "Microcomputers and Adult Education." In D. Gueulette (Ed.), *Microcomputers for Adult Learning: Potentials and Perils.* Chicago: Follett, 1982.

Naisbitt, J. *Megatrends.* New York: Warner Books, 1982.

Sheckley, B. G. "Self-Directed Learning Among Adults in a Community College." *Community and Junior College Research Quarterly,* 1985, *9* (2).

Strange, J. "Preparing for Tomorrow Today." *AAHE Bulletin,* 1983, *36* (2), 9-11.

Tough, A. *The Adult's Learning Projects: A Fresh Approach to Theory and Practice in Adult Education.* (2nd ed.). Ontario: Ontario Institute for Studies in Education, 1979.

Barry G. Sheckley is an assistant professor of education at the University of Connecticut. He serves as the New England Regional Manager for the Council for the Advancement of Experiential Learning.

Index